Grand Army Men

THE GAR AND ITS MALE ORGANIZATIONS

A Collectors Guide and History
of the
Grand Army of the Republic

Sons of Union Veterans
of the Civil War

Military Order of the Loyal
Legion

by

Robert J. Wolz

Frank Leslie September 5, 1891

Grand Army Men: the GAR and Its Male Organizations

For information please contact:
Robert Wolz, Box 1411, Key West, FL 33041. Email RJWolz@GMail.com

Key West Publishing, LLC, Key West, FL. 2014

Library of Congress Cataloging-in-Publication Data

Wolz, Robert J.
  Grand Army Men : the GAR and its male organizations : a collectors guide and history of the Grand Army of the Republic, Sons of Union Veterans of the Civil War, Military Order of the Loyal Legion / by Robert J. Wolz.
     pages cm
  Includes bibliographical references and index.
   ISBN 978-0-9778528-3-3 (alk. paper)
  1. Grand Army of the Republic--Collectibles. 2. Grand Army of the Republic--History. 3. United States--History--Civil War, 1861-1865--Collectibles. I. Title.
   E462.1.A7W65 2014
   973.7075--dc23
                                                    2014028443

        Cover Design: An adaptation of the official program for the 24th National Encampment of the Grand Army of the Republic, 1890.

A morsel of genuine history is a thing
so rare as to be always valuable.

Thomas Jefferson in a letter to John Adams 1817

DEDICATION

This work is dedicated to the Past, the Present, and to the Future.

To John Wolz, James McKean, David Barto, and Edwin Donaldson, all Pennsylvanians, who served in the Union Army and gave me my eligibility to join the Sons of Union Veterans of the Civil War.

To Carl Burcaw and Harold Huttenhower, two actual Sons who loved the Order and kept the bills paid until my younger generation came along in the early 1960s.

To Frank M. Heacock, Albert Lambert, Chester Shriver, William Coffin, Fred Combs, LeRoy Stoudt, and Richard Orr, seven outstanding Sons' Commanders-in-Chief from whom I was honored to learn so much.

To my dad, Robert C. Wolz, who served as Ohio Department Sons Commander in 1973-74.

To my sons, Jason Alexander and Grant Robert, with whom I have tried to share a love of history and the importance of family.

To a special friend, Edward Damich.

To my many friends, Brothers and Sisters, in the Allied GAR Orders, thanks for your support and encouragement.

Finally, to all of you who want to learn more about the Grand Army Family, welcome.

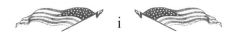

Printed in USA
CPSIA: 1-2000-14-43434

ACKNOWLEDGEMENTS

This is not the work of a single individual. Generations past have created the history I am recording.

Special thanks to those who have helped with this research, read through numerous old proceedings and minute-books and searched for badge varieties:
Gordon R. Bury, Past Commander-in-Chief, SUVCW & MOLLUS
Lynne Bury, Past National President, LGAR
Elizabeth Rock, LGAR and Robert Rock, MOLLUS
Elmer Atkinson, Past Commander-in-Chief, SUVCW
Margaret Atkinson, Past National President, ASUVCW
Jim Pahl, Past Commander-in-Chief, SUVCW
David V. Medert, Past Commander-in-Chief, SUVCW
Keith Harrison, Past Commander-in-Chief, SUVCW & MOLLUS
Jerry Orton, Past National Historian, SUVCW
Lorraine Orton, National Historian, WRC
Roger Heiple, GAR collector & historian
Gary Gibson, Past National Historian, SUVCW
Ron Bellenger, Past Michigan Department Historian, SUVCW
Argus Ogborn, Past Department Commander, Indiana SUVCW
William C. Duval, Past Commander-in-Chief, MOLLUS
Dr. Barbara Gannon, professor of Military History, University of Central Florida

To the staff of the GAR Museum and Library of Philadelphia, the Soldier and Sailors Hall of Pittsburgh, the US Army Military History Center of Carlisle, the Library of Congress, the National Archives, the National Park Service, and the American Numismatic Society for their expert help.

This work would not have been produced without the technical support of: Bob Bernreuter for layout, design, and publishing; Suellen Croteau, Everitt Bowles, Gary Gibson, and Keith Harrison for expert proofreading; and Dylan Kibler for his photographic expertise.

To the many GAR dealers and collectors who have sold me badge varieties and literature or supplied photos from their personal collections and helped me find unknown examples: Brian Hanlon, Richard Dzialo, Kenneth Johnson, Joe Moore , Karen Mysliviec, George G. Kane, Ed Strobridge, Dennis Gregg, Tom MacDonald, Noel Preston, Everitt Bowles, Joe Mitrovich, Francis Frederick, Don Wagner and my many internet friends and contacts who have radically changed collecting...bringing forth items not found in 50 years of visiting antique shops. Thank you.

ABOUT THE AUTHOR

Robert J. Wolz was born in June 1946. He graduated with a degree in American history from Youngstown State University. He has completed postgraduate work at the University of Central Florida. In 2014, he serves as the Executive Director of the Harry S. Truman Little White House Museum and State Heritage Landmark in Key West, Florida and is the Executive Director of the Key West Harry S. Truman Foundation.

He has previously written articles on the American presidency, co-authored *Presidents in Paradise: The Legacy of the Little White House* and co-edited *The National Security Legacy of Harry S. Truman* and *Israel and the Legacy of Harry S Truman* and numerous articles in *The Banner,* journal of the Sons of Union Veterans of the Civil War.

His interest in American history began in his early teen years and he began attending a Camp of the Sons of Union Veterans of the Civil War when he was 15.

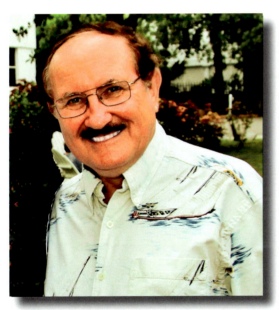

He was inducted into membership shortly after his 16th birthday. He served every office in Philip Triem Camp #43, every office in the Department of Ohio except Department Secretary-Treasurer and every office in the National Organization of the Sons except Commander-in-Chief and National Secretary-Treasurer. He is Life Member # 61 in the Sons of Union Veterans of the Civil War. His eligibility is based upon the Civil War service of two great-grandfathers and several great-uncles. Two were killed in action or died of their wounds. Two great-grandfathers were members of the GAR and his mother and father were also active in the Allied GAR Orders. He was a youthful Civil War re-enactor and enlisted in the 19th Ohio Regiment, SVR in 1963. Eventually, he served as the Quartermaster General and the Adjutant General, National Military Department, Sons of Veterans Reserve. He counted among his close friends a number of Sons who had joined 50 to 60 years before. This rare opportunity allowed him access to information that might have been lost. In addition to the Sons of Union Veterans, he holds membership in the Sons of the American Revolution, The General Society of the War of 1812 and the Military Order of the Loyal Legion of the United States.

He has two sons, Jason and Grant, and is active in his community and church. He is the recipient of the Vigil Honor from the Order of the Arrow, the Silver Beaver from South Florida Council, Boy Scouts of America and the Order of St. George.

He holds professional membership in the American Alliance of Museums, the American Association for State and Local History, the Florida Association of Museums and the Florida Trust for Historic Preservation.

While he has collected for more than 50 years, fifteen years of research and contributions by a number of national officers in the Allied Orders have made this work possible.

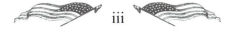

Leland J. Webb
One of the Boys in Blue

Leland Webb was a son of a veteran and a veteran as well. He enlisted on October 15, 1861 at the age of 15 and served the next four years. After the war he had a distinguished career as an attorney, mayor of his town and a member of the United States House of Representatives.

He served as Aide-de-Camp to GAR Commander John Rea in 1888 and was responsible for introducing the resolutions giving Grand Army recognition to the Sons of Veterans, USA. He served as the Sons' Commander-in-Chief 1890-1891. This photograph shows him wearing the Gold Star awarded for meritorious service, his Past Division Commander's badge, his four star rank as the sitting Commander-in-Chief and his Grand Army of the Republic badge. Missing from this photo is his Gold Cross as Past Grand Division Commander.

TABLE OF CONTENTS

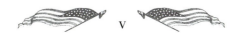

INTRODUCTION

This book is about the Grand Army of the Republic, the GAR, the organization formed by the Union veterans of the Civil War in 1866 and about their sons. A brief history is given in this book and then a collector's guide to their badges and insignia. While other topics of collecting are touched upon, the major focus of this book is the membership and officers' badges of these organizations. ***Grand Army Men: the GAR and Its Male Organizations*** is a work in progress.

A great deal of new research is offered for the use of the beginner, intermediate or advanced collector and the membership of these Orders, but this work could cover thousands of pages and it still would not be complete.

Lynn J. Shaw, Commander-in-Chief of the Sons of Confederate Veterans 1984-86, felt this same inadequacy when he attempted to catalog the United Confederate Veterans and Sons of Confederate Veterans badges. He states, "With local, regional, state and national groups within each organization, all commemorating the war and its participants at different times and places, one can begin to see how varied are the remaining representations of ribbons and badges. It is sad to note how many of these mementoes have been lost to us for all time simply out of neglect or indifference."[1]

This book will help members and collectors recognize badges and mementoes produced over the last 149 years by the members of the Grand Army of the Republic and their Sons. The common abbreviations will be used throughout this book rather than spell out the full name each time. The Grand Army or GAR refers to the Grand Army of the Republic. The Sons of Veterans or Sons of Union Veterans of the Civil War is called the Sons, SV or SUVCW. The Military Order of the Loyal Legion of the United States was not one of the GAR affiliated organizations, but very closely allied with it and for that reason is included in this book. They are commonly referred to as the Loyal Legion or MOLLUS.

This book attempts for the first time to place in sequential order all the membership badges of each of the Orders.

There may be unrecorded and forgotten varieties of badges and medals not

shown or listed here. Information presented in this text represents our best guess today.

Please share information on any unknown variety so that it will not be lost to future generations. Numerous official sources, usually not available to non-members of these organizations, are quoted so members and collectors can appreciate differences within each organization and each collection.

As with any antique collection, each individual will have to create the parameters of his or her collection. Several million Americans have belonged to the GAR and their Allied Orders: the Sons of Union Veterans, Daughters of Union Veterans, the Woman's Relief Corps, and Ladies of the GAR or Auxiliary to the Sons. This means that millions of badges, ribbons, pins, jewelry and souvenirs were produced. Some items are very plentiful even after 149 years and readily available to all. Some items are extremely rare and can only to be found after years of searching, lots of good luck and perhaps spending a small fortune. Never expect completeness as it will only lead to discouragement.

On the other hand, there are many specialized topics for the collector such as, National Encampment souvenir badges, patriotic postcards issued for the GAR, for Memorial Day or the Fourth of July and official GAR and Allied Orders stationery and these could make a colorful and provocative collection. Stamp collectors might be interested in the First Day of Issue covers of Scott's #985, the last encampment of the GAR, issued in 1949 as well as earlier reunion and encampment commemorative covers. Of course, vintage clothing advocates will not be disappointed with the large variety of hats, coats, belts, swords or canes to collect. Ephemera collectors will delight at the volume of printed materials: journals, proceedings, membership certificates and cards, prints and photographs, books, regulations, constitutions, rituals and accounts that offer glimpses of America's past and should be lovingly preserved for future generations. The number of topics available to collectors is incredible. Most likely, you own several pieces and thus your interest in this book.

This brings up the inevitable question of "What is it worth? What should I pay?"

These items are worth what you and other collectors are willing to pay for them. Prices have steadily gone up. GAR collecting is considered a popular collectible today and many GAR items may be overpriced based upon the quantities produced, but items from the Allied Orders seem to be underpriced and not yet appreciated. Your location and the item's scarcity, condition and demand among collectors all control prices. Price guides, antique shows and the internet are educating most interested persons. Consider the fact that 409,489 men belonged to the GAR in the year 1890 alone. Many more men belonged and dropped out before and after this date and each was issued a membership badge. In addition to these, there are numerous official Post, Department and National badges issued which means in excess of several million badges were produced during the life of the GAR.

Perhaps as many as 50% were destroyed with the passage of time. Based upon quantity produced, what is a GAR badge worth? Most collectors would say $100.00 or less based upon the prices seen in antique shops or online auctions. On the other hand, what is a one-of-a-kind Past Commander-in-Chief of the GAR badge worth? Only eighty-two men ever held the office. While multiple badges could have been created as testimonials, the number remains quite small. These were usually custom-made works of art handcrafted in gold with precious or semi-precious gems by the finest jewelers. This makes it truly a Holy Grail to seek, and perhaps just as hard to find!

A word about convention badges. The GAR, the Woman's Relief Corps and Ladies of the GAR held their national and state conventions in the same city and on the same date. The Daughters of Union Veterans held their conventions with the GAR even before they were officially recognized in 1900. The Sons of Union Veterans and their Auxiliary met in a different city and on a different date from the GAR. The Sons were a military organization and were encamped in the field at a different location, but they always sent large delegations to the GAR National Encampment. Thus, the collector may discover two Sons National Convention badges for the same year: one for the Sons National Encampment and one as a representative to the GAR National Encampment. For example, the GAR met September 12-13, 1901 in Cleveland, Ohio. Official delegate badges to the GAR Encampment were 1600 for Grand Army delegates, 550 for the Woman's Relief Corps, 400 for the Ladies of GAR, 150 for the Daughters of Veterans, 1350 for the Sons of Veterans, and 150 for the Sons Auxiliary. On September 17-18, 1901, the Sons and their auxiliary held their own convention in Providence, Rhode Island, and they produced a similar number of badges for their own encampment. From 1910 through 1949, all the Allied Orders usually met in the same city and on the same dates. The Woman's Relief Corps and the Daughters of Union Veterans of the Civil War have met independently of the other three Orders since 1950.

The GAR and Sons continued to use the term "encampment" from the days when they camped in tents in the field. The women's orders usually use the term "convention" for their state and national meetings.

NATIONAL ENCAMPMENT of the G.A.R.
Near Minneapolis Harvester Works
MINNEAPOLIS, MINN. JULY 1884.

Frank Leslie September 5, 1891

So that the future may learn from the past.

Key West

PUBLISHING, LLC

X

Basic Collecting

As you start to put together a collection of badges, ribbons and Grand Army collectibles you should be aware of several important factors.

Examine the Details

The differences between varieties of badge types can be ***VERY small***. Buy a good magnifier or jeweler's loupe. Using this magnifier, you will be able to read the fine print of the manufacturer's names and patent dates or locate the hallmark of the manufacturer.

Careful Handling

Handle with care. Oils and dirt from your hands can stain the cloth ribbons and mar photographs and prints and, over time, even etch the metal of badges. Wash your hands before examining your "treasures". You might even consider wearing cotton gloves.

Cleaning & Polishing Badges

Metal parts of badges may be gently cleaned using cotton swabs, soft cloth, a soft tooth brush with a little mild soap and water. Dry completely. Should you decide to use a polish, NEVER use cleaners/polish containing abrasives, acids or bleach. Do not use "dip" cleaners like Tarn-X ® as they will remove the original finish and leave your antique badge looking like a new shiny penny.

Many badges had a chemically created finish. The finish was sprayed on, then baked, thus creating a uniform bronze finish. Joseph Davison, the official jeweler of most of the GAR Orders, even patented a "chocolate velvet" finish. It is best to test the cleaner or polish on the back. Use it very sparingly; a little less is better than too much. Once the years of grime are removed, store the badge away.

Proper Storage

Protect your investment. Store badges separately. Throwing them in a shoe box may have been fine when you were a child, but you are now the guardian of history. Badges rubbing against each other scratch the surface of the metal and add dirt to the ribbons. Store them individually in plastic bags, plastic boxes or butterfly collecting boxes. Whenever possible, wrap each in acid free tissue paper. Do not

1

allow them to be stored on foam rubber (even if that is how you received them). Foam rubber releases sulfur and will destroy your badges. Throw it out! I recently found a box of Civil War Centennial commemorative badges I earned as a youthful re-enactor. Each was "protected" in a plastic box with foam rubber padding. The surface in contact with the foam rubber was pitted and tarnished green. This is less than desirable, to be sure, and unfortunately not repairable.

If you have a quantity of badges and ribbons, consider dusting each well and wrapping each in acid free tissue paper and storing them in a box. Photographs and printed materials should be cleaned and put into Mylar or plastic page protectors for storage. I recommend a dry cleaning pad to remove dust and surface contaminates. Don't use an eraser or you may erase what you are trying to protect.

Remember: light, moisture, chemical contaminates and vermin are the four problems from which to protect your collection. Sunlight and bright direct light fade ribbons and printing inks, and dry out silk ribbon. Roof leaks can cause water stains. Too much moisture around your collection leads to mold and foxing in printed materials. Air-conditioned homes are best for proper storage. Ideal conditions call for 65° to 70° Fahrenheit with 45% to 55% relative humidity.

Rubber bands and foam rubber as well as various tape residues dry out leaving discolorations, pitting, and sticky spots that you cannot remove. Also avoid harsh cleaners and solvents; most collectors prefer the patina developed on the badges with time. Polishing them actually can lessen the value by 75%.

Vermin (yes, we are talking about bugs and mice) can be a major problem. Cockroaches, silverfish, bookworms, mites, termites, and moths love old paper and will eat the finish off photographs and make holes in your book's pages. Mice have been known to chew books and ribbons or nest in old mementos stored in the attic, basement or garage.

Display

If you have a limited number of badges, you might consider mounting them in shadowbox frames. There are a few concerns to consider if you chose to display them on the wall or in a table top. Keep them out of direct sunlight as the ribbons will fade quickly and the inks used in cello badges and photos will discolor. DO NOT USE GLUE; it will permanently ruin your badges. In the past, some collectors used straight pins to pin them to the backing; over time, most pins rust or tarnish discoloring the ribbons on your badges. Do not pad your frame with foam rubber (see section above!). Ask your framing store for acid free products or museum

preservation materials. One option is to sew the badge in three spots to the backing. (Two at the bar pin, one at the ring between the pendant and ribbon) Lapel pins, rosettes and pins can be pushed directly into the core-foam backing. It is best to use Plexiglas in the frames as it reduces harmful ultraviolet light that cause fading. Several commercial companies provide this type of mounting service for veteran's medals and come highly recommended.

Prints, certificates or photographs should be placed on acid-free backing using acid-free mat so that the glass does not touch the print. Use Plexiglas instead of regular glass as it keeps 93% of harmful ultraviolet rays out. Do not hang in bright light. Single-sheet printed materials and photographs should be cleaned and stored in polypropylene or Mylar plastic often called "page protectors" and available at office supply stores. Use acid free backing or mat boards. Store in acid free file folders. Use white backing instead of colored papers as their dyes can bleed color.

Never laminate paper items! While it may protect the item from certain environmental conditions, it uses heat & chemicals that cause the paper to deteriorate from within. Family heirlooms we laminated twenty years ago are now dark brown unreadable mementoes sealed in plastic forever.

Never use liquid plastics that pour over the paper or badges forming a hard plastic surface over them. These processes are impossible to reverse. I highly recommend A*n Ounce of Preservation: A guide to the care of papers and photographs* (ISBN # 1-56825-021-5) for its in-depth suggestions for proper care of all paper items.

Buy the Best (Three things determine value: scarcity, demand, and condition.)

Scarcity: How many were made? Many membership badges were manufactured in the tens of thousands. They are more than 100 years old, but the quantity made should keep them reasonably priced. Five varieties of the same design may exist, and certain varieties may be rarer and sought by the specialized collector. If you desire to be a specialist, study so that you can spot the rare varieties from the commonplace.

Demand: The Civil War Centennial has brought perhaps a million new collectors and many new dealers to our field. The sesquicentennial of the Civil War will bring a million more collectors into the field. While it is unlikely that the demand will lessen, perhaps, through education, the marketplace will stabilize with a lowering of prices on the commonplace and bring a true value to the unique items that are rarely offered.

Condition, condition, condition: Buy the best example you can find. While it is difficult to find mint, fresh-from-the-manufacturer examples and you'll pay top price if you do, buy the best specimen you can afford. Do not buy poor quality or damaged items because they are cheap. Remember what your grandmother always told you: "You get what you pay for."

Badge Ribbons

Ribbons are the most troublesome area in badge collecting. The metal parts of the badge last, the ribbon does not.

In a few cases, like the general membership badge of the Woman's Relief Corps, the badge has a red, white, and blue striped ribbon that is readily obtainable. Reproduction ribbons of the officer's flag ribbons of the GAR, Ladies of the GAR, and Daughters of Union Veterans have recently been reproduced. As a last resort to replacing the ribbon, you might consider washing it. Some ribbons can be safely washed in cold water and pressed, some ribbons bleed color. Test wash a spot on back. As a general rule, please DO NOT REPLACE the original ribbon with a ribbon you found at the florist or craft store. If possible, contact a supplier for badges to buy the correct weight, size and color and replace the ribbon with the same ribbon you are removing. It should cost less than $10.00 and often they will correctly "re-drape" the badge (replace the ribbon and reattach the clasp). I have seen numerous badges offered for sale with some strange ribbons on them. This is a disservice to history. Future generations will be trying to figure out why the Sons of Union Veterans used lime green ribbon on some of their badges when, in fact, they never did.

Some collectors believe you should always leave the badge in "found condition." If the ribbon is falling off, it stays falling off. Personally, I believe we honor the veterans and Allied Orders members by presenting the badge in its best possible condition, not its worst. If you belong to the Allied GAR Orders, contact your headquarters for a replacement ribbon. The Sons of Union Veterans still use the same distinctive ribbon today as they have since 1882. If it's faded, dirty, and worn, buy an official replacement ribbon. All the Allied Orders have regulations stating you should replace ribbons as they become soiled or faded.

Silk Ribbon Badges

Silk memorial badges or ribbons are becoming rare because the silk dries out and becomes extremely fragile. Any unnecessary handling causes splits and breaks. Sometimes the badge will fall apart in your hands. Usually these should be stored between two pieces of polyethylene or in special plastic envelopes used to store

archival materials. Never glue them in books. Never attach them with tape. The silk ribbon will be damaged and the badge destroyed. They cannot be repaired once damaged. Condition has everything to do with this collectible. Originally in the 1890s, they sold for $1.20 to $3.00 per dozen. Today, fancy double-faced badges or those with two or three layers of silk and cello buttons attached can be $30.00 to $75.00 each. In good condition, these are some of the rarer Grand Army collectibles because of their fragile condition.

Insurance

If your collection just consists of the badge or two you were presented, your homeowner's policy should cover its replacement. Collections, however, tend to grow and increase in value quickly... especially if you pay $25.00 per badge and you own several hundred badges. Recently, a collection was appraised that was bought over several years, one piece at a time, and the value exceeded $50,000.

Protect your collection from theft and other losses by insuring it. You must call your insurance company and tell them you have $ xxxx in antiques and need it insured. Your homeowner's insurance policy usually will not cover losses over $250 unless you bought the added protection. Some insurance agents may have to find a specialized policy for you, such as those offered by Chubbs. Whatever you do, do not assume it is covered unless you have asked your insurance agent.

Stolen Property

This book deals with the personal possessions of the members of the Grand Army of the Republic and their Allied Orders. Due to the tremendous increases in the value of Civil War artifacts and former Grand Army possessions, items are being stolen from public buildings and displays. These items usually are owned by the Allied Orders of the GAR or its legal heir, the Sons of Union Veterans. Some items are clearly corporate possessions. No individual ever "owned" the charters, corporate seals, or Letters of Patent of one of the GAR Orders. While it could be argued that someone "saved" these items from destruction, the truth is they should be returned to the national organizations and not sold on internet auctions or in antique shops.

Grave Markers and War Memorials

While bronze grave markers (the star that held the American flag by the head stones) have been eliminated from many cemeteries with flat headstones, still many are being stolen from cemeteries either for their metal value or by relic hunters selling them to collectors. In many states, these bronze grave markers were purchased with tax dollars and are regarded as government property. Grave markers are provided for all deceased veterans under provisions of the County Code or Veterans Affairs. The most common type is an upright bronze marker bearing a service medallion, which also functions as a holder for a small American flag. The cost of both original and replacement markers is borne by county government. Their sale is illegal. Personally, I would recommend you not collect any of these items so as to discourage further thefts.

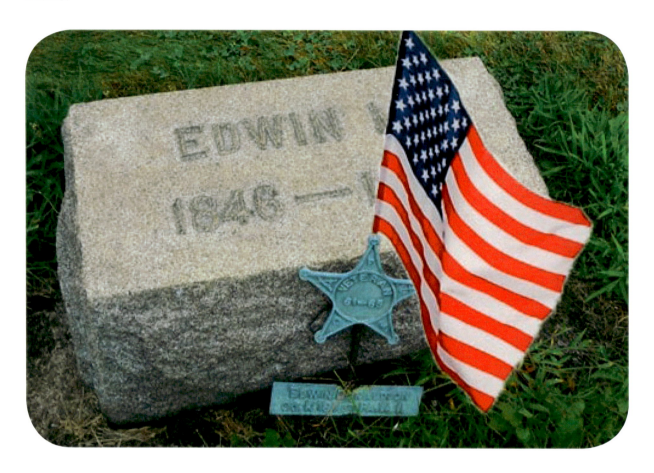

My great-grandfather Edwin M. Donaldson's grave site,
Grandview Cemetery, East Palestine, Ohio.

"For every veteran's marker that is stolen or purchased at an auction or flea market, a veteran is being denied the honor of a flag at his or her final resting place."   Former Pennsylvania Governor Tom Ridge May 4, 2001

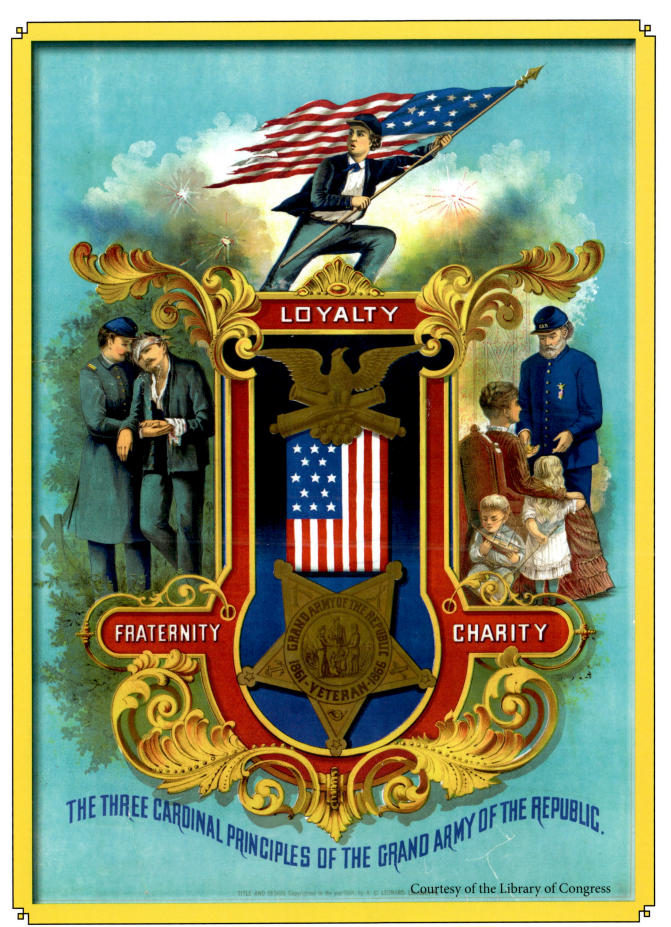

LOYALTY

FRATERNITY

CHARITY

GRAND ARMY OF THE REPUBLIC
1861 · VETERAN · 1866

THE THREE CARDINAL PRINCIPLES OF THE GRAND ARMY OF THE REPUBLIC.

TITLE AND DESIGN Copyrighted in the year 1884, by A. C. LEONARD,

THE OLD GRAND ARMY BOYS

Henry J. Cummings, Muskegon, MI

Presented by Frank M. Heacock, Sons' Commander-in-Chief
at the Grand Army Campfire Program in 1969.

You may talk about the Masons
And the Odd Fellows and such:
You may call them so fraternal
As to fairly beat the Dutch.
You may praise them if you choose
With their mystic rites and noise
But they can not hold a candle
To the Old Grand Army Boys.

For a man that has the money
Can learn all about their Craft;
He can get degrees and passwords
That would make a funeral laugh
And be loaded down with symbols
But for true fraternal joys
They can not hold a candle
To the Old Grand Army Boys.

They may talk about their badges
But the one that has the call
Is the Star and Flag and Eagle
Which is far above them all.
It was won where cannon thundered
Mid the battle's smoke and noise
So there's nothing holds a candle
To the Old Grand Army Boys.

Why ? They fought and bled together
And they shared the prison's pen
They faced the front in battle
With the manly touch of men.
Then the compact was cemented
Mid the conflict's crash and noise
So there is nothing holds a candle
To the Old Grand Army Boys.

They fraternal? Well, I reckon:
And their charity is all right.
Are they loyal? They have proved it
For they left their homes to fight;
And this nation owes them homage
For the peace it now enjoys!
So there is nothing holds a candle
To the Old Grand Army Boys!

An Order to include all honorably discharged Union Veterans.

An Introductory History to the Grand Army of the Republic and Its Male Organizations

Albert Woolson
last GAR veteran

Bruce Catton, writing a eulogy in *Life Magazine* for Albert Woolson the last Union veteran, who died on August 2, 1956, put it this way: "The Grand Army of the Republic has marched off to join the shadows, and no matter how long the nation exists there will never be anything quite like it again. This chapter in our history is closed. Something deeply and fundamentally American is gone forever.

"For the Grand Army of the Republic was the living link that bound us intimately to the great morning of national youth. As long as the Army existed, even though it was at last embodied in one incredibly old man, who stood without comrades, the great day of tragedy and of decision was still a part of living memory. There was an

 9

open door into the past, and what we could see through that opening was magically haunted, because everything that was visible there was strangely touched by the light of the future."[2]

The American Civil War was the greatest tragedy in our history. More Americans were involved in this war than all other wars because, sadly, we were at war with ourselves. More than four million Americans took up arms against each other.

Author William Price writing at the time of the Civil War Centennial noted the Civil War holds "...a place in history midway between the Revolutionary War of the 18th century and the First World War of the 20th. The American Civil War had far reaching effects: by the many innovations and developments it stimulated, it became the forerunner of modern warfare; by the demands it made on technology and production, it hastened the industrial revolution in America... and emerging from such trying times were five future Presidents of the United States, all officers of the Union Army"[3] and members of the Grand Army of the Republic.

The vast majority of those involved on both sides of the war were young men between the ages of 16 and 23. In the north, they truly were the "Boys in Blue".

From April 12, 1861, to the close of the war on April 9, 1865, it is recorded that 2,778,304 boys and men enlisted in the Union Army. The statistics of the youngest enlistments are recorded here.

Those 10 years of age and under……...…………….25

Those 11 years of age…………………………….38

Those 12 years of age…………………....……...225

Those 13 years of age ………...……………...…...300

Those 14 years of age…………………….……1523

Those 15 years of age………………….……104,987

Those 16 years of age………………....…....231,051

Those 17 years of age…………………...…..844,981

Those 18 years of age……………………….1,151,438[4]

Youthful black and white Federal sailors onboard Ironclad Hunchback (National Archives)

These young men grew up in the defense of the country, and the comradeship of war was not to be forgotten. In the final months of the Civil War, many discussions arose about life after the war. Who would provide for the disabled? Who would care for the widows and orphans? Who would honor the dead? Was the rebellion really ended or would the South rise again?

With the surrender of Robert E. Lee to U.S. Grant on April 9, 1865, the rebellion was officially over. More than a million men were discharged and returned to civilian life. Most did not want to break the ties of kinship welded from the shared experiences of war.

Robert Beath

As early as April 15, 1865, Union officers met in Philadelphia to form an Honor Guard following President Lincoln's assassination. This was the first great Civil War veterans' society to form. This organization is called the Military Order of the Loyal Legion of the United States. It is also known as MOLLUS or the Loyal Legion.[5] Although not a member of the Allied GAR Orders, almost all the Loyal Legion members were active in the GAR; for this reason a brief history of the Loyal Legion is presented in a later chapter of this book and their badges are illustrated. According to Robert Beath in his 1888 History of the Grand Army of the Republic, at their first national encampment the GAR adopted the titles of officers, general organizational plan and the principles of Loyalty from the Loyal Legion.[6]

The Grand Review of Federal troops at war's end. (Library of Congress)

As a final act together, more than 150,000 victorious Federal troops marched down Pennsylvania Avenue in Washington, DC on May 23 and 24, 1865. Major General Joshua Lawrence Chamberlain captured the moment when he said, "The pageant has passed. The day is over. But we linger, loath to think we shall see them no more together – these men, these horses, these Colors afield."

Within months of the war's conclusion, numerous reunion organizations began to form. The Society of the Army of the Potomac, the Society of the Army of the Cumberland, the Society of the Army of the Tennessee, the Union Veterans'

Legion, the Union Veterans' Union, the Ex-Prisoners of War Association, are examples. Each of these reunion organizations had its own specialized requirements for admission based upon former corps affiliation, length of service, pension or political interests[7] and most had their own badges. The Grand Army of the Republic was different in that it was to be an Order to include **all** honorably discharged Union Veterans.

Major Benjamin Franklin Stephenson, MD, was the sole organizer of the Grand Army of the Republic. His organization was to be all-encompassing and to be all-inclusive to honorably discharged Union veterans.[8]

Benjamin F. Stephenson,
founder. GAR

The First Twelve
Grand Army Men

Decatur Post #1

Instituted April 6, 1866

(Robert Beath's 1888 History of The Grand Army of the Republic)

For nearly a year, organizational plans were made with vast amounts of correspondence between Stephenson and his former comrades. A ritual was designed, a constitution written, the basis of a national organization laid, charters created and on April 6, 1866, Decatur, Illinois, Post # 1 was instituted with a dozen members. Post # 2 soon followed in Springfield, Illinois.

Organizational work continued by Dr. Stephenson, even to the neglect of his medical practice and his family and in November, 1866, a national meeting was called in Indianapolis, Indiana, with representatives from Illinois, Missouri, Kansas, Wisconsin, Ohio, Pennsylvania, New York, Kentucky, Iowa, Indiana, and the District of Columbia present.

As founder, Dr. Stephenson called the meeting to order as Commander-in-Chief and appointed a "Committee upon Permanent Organization". John Palmer, the Illinois Department Commander, presided at this organizational meeting. Two hundred and twenty-eight delegates attended. General Stephen A. Hurlbut was elected Commander-in-Chief. Dr. Stephenson

S. A. Hurlbut, first elected
GAR Commander-in-Chief

was elected the Adjutant General. He never served as an elected Commander-in-Chief as he died in 1871.[9]

Membership requirements were simple. A candidate had to be a man of good moral character, have an honorable discharge from the Union Army stating his military service was between April 12, 1861 and April 9, 1865, and that he never bore arms against the federal government.

No veteran could enlist in the Grand Army unless he was elected into membership in his local post. If he moved, he had to request a "transfer" to his new post and he had to request an "honorable discharge" to leave the Order. Breaches of discipline could result in a "courts martial" resulting in a "dishonorable discharge".

A candidate was elected using the Masonic voting system of black and white balls.[10] Trescott Post 10 of the GAR in Salem, Ohio had a typical ballot box consisting of two drawers in a box on the bottom with a carved cannon barrel on top. One drawer was filled with black and white marbles. The second chamber was empty to receive the balloting balls.

Each member advanced to the Altar, saluted the Commander, then selected a ball and "loaded" the cannon. The ball would roll down the barrel and drop into the empty chamber below casting his vote.

Ballot Box

When all members had voted, the Post Commander would examine the ballots declaring the candidate elected or rejected. If the candidate was "black-balled" receiving four negative votes in twenty, the rejection was noted in a "black list" book and published in general orders. He could not re-apply for membership. If the candidate was elected into membership, ritualistic work would follow exemplifying the lessons of Fraternity, Charity, and Loyalty. (F, C, and L) the guiding principles of the GAR. Short allegorical plays often portraying camp life and sometimes augmented with "magic lantern" slides depicting battle and patriotic scenes were performed.[11] A member was usually greeted by the term, "Comrade"; the exception was for posts made up of naval veterans who could refer to each other as "Shipmate".[12]

The Grand Army post room was of standard design and used with little variation by all its Allied Orders. In the center of the room was an altar and around it, all ritual was performed. The altar was covered with the American flag, an open Bible placed upon the flag, and crossed swords placed on top of the Bible. Members were seated around the sides of the room. In front of the altar stood the position of the Post Commander, flanked

Interior view of post 2 Philadelphia

by the Post Adjutant (Secretary) and Post Quartermaster (Treasurer). Opposite the Commander was the Post Senior Vice Commander (Vice President), to the right was the position of the Junior Vice Commander, and to the left the Chaplain's position.

Guards were posted at the inner and outer doors, and admission was only granted to members possessing the proper password and counter-signs.

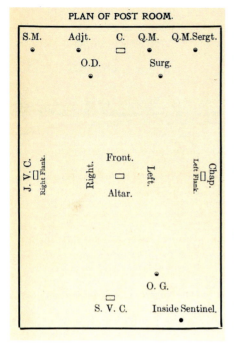

The Post room created an imaginary replica of an army post.[13] Ten duly elected comrades were needed to form a local "Post". The post could be named for a deceased veteran, a battle, or the town's name, or occasionally, an Army nurse. The physical "post" might be a series of rented rooms above a storefront or an entire building occupying a position of importance on the town square and designated as a "Memorial Hall". No duplicate names were allowed for posts within a Department (usually one state, but could represent adjoining states if membership numbers did not warrant creating separate state organizations.) Officers, past commanders and elected representatives represented the "Post" at the annual state convention called the "Department Encampment".

Memorial Hall of Topeka, Kansas

Department Commanders, Past Department Commanders and elected representatives represented the state in the national convention or encampment. The "National Encampment" was the supreme authority in the operation of the organization. Between sessions of the National Encampment, a board of directors consisting of the elected national officers and a Council of Administration would conduct the affairs of the organization.[14]

While politics was strictly forbidden within the posts, the Republican Party candidates often had the Grand Army's support. So much so the GAR was once referred to as the "Grand Army of the Republicans" by political pundits. In 1952, a study by Mary Dearing entitled *Veterans in Politics: The Story of the GAR* referred to the Grand Army as "cogs in the Republican machine".[15] The use of the GAR by the Republicans actually hurt the organization in its early years as it was perceived, perhaps rightfully so, as a political organization and numerous members dropped out.[16]

In an attempt to imitate other popular men's fraternities such as the Masonic Lodge, the Odd Fellows, or the Knights of Pythias, the GAR tried to establish a degree system of recruit, soldier, and veteran. This also resulted in the closing of numerous posts as these former soldiers refused to retake lower degrees.[17] The Grand Army of the Republic was off to a very uncertain beginning.

General John A. Logan was elected Commander-in-Chief in 1868. He erected the first amphitheater at Arlington Cemetery that year. As both an outstanding military strategist and masterful politician, he knew the value of the military vote for himself and his Republican allies. He ran for Vice President in 1884 with James Blaine as the Republican presidential candidate against Democrat Grover Cleveland. He never failed to remind his listeners that while "not all Democrats were rebels, all rebels had been Democrats."

John A. Logan

However, he is best remembered for his now famous General Orders #11 Series of 1868 creating Memorial Day to honor the fallen comrades, the bivouac of the dead. May 30th was to be set aside to decorate the graves of their former comrades and soldiers.[18] For this reason, the holiday was originally called Decoration Day in most communities.

Color post card of Decoration Day in Sandusky, Ohio

Permanent monuments made of stone or metal were erected in nearly every northern city as a reminder of the sacrifices of the veterans to preserve the Union. In 1878, the Grand Army erected some of the first monuments on the Gettysburg battlefield. [19]

The members of the GAR were largely white, two-thirds were native born and from lower middle class to middle class families. The other third of the Union army were immigrants. These immigrants were mostly Irish, German, Dutch, English, French, and Canadian in the east and Hispanic in the west. Approximately twenty percent of the army was German, thus some GAR Posts conducted the ritual totally in German, such as the August Willich Post 195 of Cincinnati, Ohio.

The shared experience of war, the idea that their comrades-in-arms had shared a morsel of food in the prison camp or a few drops of water on the battlefield under scorching heat created familial bonds as close as blood kinship or marriage.

A recurring iconic theme emerged to express this fraternity: "We Drank From The Same Canteen."

Badges, ribbons, and physical small canteens fashioned in metal and ceramics as well as representations on paper were lasting souvenirs of Department and National Encampments.

The Same Canteen

Charles Graham Halpin (1829-1868)

Written under the name Pvt Miles O'Reiley, 47th NY Infantry

There are bonds of all sorts in this world of ours,
Fetters of friendship and ties of flowers,
And true lover's knots, I ween;
The girl and the boy are bound by a kiss,
But there's never a bond, old friend, like this,
We have drank from the same Canteen!

It was sometimes water, and sometimes milk,
And sometimes apple-jack "fine as silk;"
But whatever the tipple has been
We shared it together in bane or bliss,
And I warm to you, friend, when I think of this,
We drank from the same Canteen!

The rich and great sit down to dine,
They quaff to each other in sparkling wine,
From glasses of crystal and green;
But I guess in their golden potations they miss
The warmth of regard to be found in this,
We drank from the same Canteen!

We have shared our blankets and tents together,
And have marched and fought in all kinds of weather,
And hungry and full we have been;
Had days of battle and days of rest,
But this memory I cling to and love the best,
We drank from the same Canteen!

For when wounded I lay on the center slope,
With my blood flowing fast and so little hope
Upon which my faint spirit could lean;
Oh! then I remember you crawled to my side,
And bleeding so fast it seemed both must have died,
We drank from the same Canteen!

All were considered equal in their Grand Army membership.

William Warner, Commander-in-Chief in 1889, in his report to the National Encampment, states: "the general and the private, the merchant prince and the clerk, the millionaire and the laborer, sit side by side as comrades, bound each to the other, by ties the tenderest yet most enduring of any in the world, outside the family circle."[20]

When Fort Sumter was fired upon "enslaved people made themselves free by rushing to the United States armies at the very first chance, beginning in May 1861, before the first battle, when three (black) men risked their lives to serve under General Benjamin F. Butler at Fort Monroe."[21] Over the next four years 180,000 African-Americans served in the United States Army and 18,000 in the U.S. Navy and they were also eligible for membership in the Grand Army.

African-American veteran
from Washington, D.C.
(Courtesy of the Library of Congress)

Posts and auxiliaries were segregated in some cases[22] as was most of American society at that time. Black veterans sometimes chose to form all black posts in cities where a large number of black veterans were present. However, the Grand Army of the Republic was the first large interracial organization in America and provided far greater acceptance of minorities than did most of society at the time. Dr. Barbara Gannon in her book, *The Won Cause: Black and White Comradeship in the Grand Army of the Republic*, (ISBN:139780807834527), cites many examples of white veterans expressing their pride in the racial composition of the Grand Army. The 1883 Missouri Department Commander is quoted, "In the Grand Army of the Republic there are no generals or privates, no distinction of race, but all are comrades."[23]

The Arkansas Department Commander in his annual report in 1905 made even a stronger declaration: "I love the GAR, when I meet a man wearing the GAR button I do not stop to see if he is dressed in broadcloth or if he has a pair of overalls, neither do I care whether he is black or white. I only see back of the button the man who had the courage to enlist as a soldier and risk his life in defense of our glorious country."[24]

Ultimately, the majority of members were white and they could have voted exclusion of African-American veterans had they so chosen. They chose instead to recognize the overwhelming shared experience of war and the stated wish of Dr. Stephenson to make the GAR **all inclusive** in spite of the racial differences.

In some of the southern states, local posts of all black or all white veterans existed. However, the Departments and National Organization were integrated. The Departments of Texas, Alabama and Mississippi attempted to form separate white and black departments within their states.

On August 7, 1891 the National Encampment of the GAR settled the question of separate "colored" departments with the following resolution: "This organization, The Grand Army of the Republic, from its birth in Decatur, Illinois, in 1866, to this, its silver encampment, has never turned from its post doors any deserving comrade, however humble, on account of his nationality, creed, or color. The only qualification for membership is an honorable discharge from the United States Army, Navy, or Marine Corps of 1861 to 1865, as the evidence that he aided in maintaining the honor, integrity, and supremacy of the National Government during the late rebellion, providing, always, that the African has done nothing in civil life to cast a stain on his honorable record in liberty's cause. During that fierce struggle for the life of the nation, we stood shoulder to shoulder as comrades tried. It is too late to divide on the color line. A man, who is good enough to stand between the flag and those who would destroy it, when the fate of the nation was trembling in the balance, is good enough to be a comrade in any department of the Grand Army of the Republic."[25] The resolution carried and the race issue was officially settled.[26] Clearly, the Grand Army was interracial because the veterans wanted it to be.

At the 1949 final encampment of the GAR, African-American Comrade Joseph Clovese of Michigan was one of the last six members attending.

Integrated Smith Post 83, Norwich NY May 30, 1897 (Library of Congress)

Many photographs of posts exist showing the Color Bearer to be African-American. Seen here is Smith Post 83 of Norwich, NY on Memorial Day 1897. Clearly the white majority was announcing to the world their pride in liberating an entire race of people.

In their early days, the members focused their efforts on their own hometown, and their relief efforts focused on local soldiers and their families (fraternity). They were a local men's lodge providing for the social and economic needs of their local members. They networked and encouraged the hiring of veterans over civilians. They had little interest in the state or national organizations. Often they failed to file any reports for months or years at a time. This was a financial disaster for the Grand Army of the Republic.

As the Grand Army focused its role more on veterans' benefits and pensions, providing care and support for disabled veterans, their widows and orphans (charity), and the teaching of patriotism (loyalty) in the public schools,

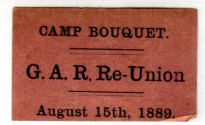

To the Commander and Comrades of _____ G. A. R _____
Post, Department of Ohio, G. A. R.

Comrades W. H. Vodrey, J. C. McIntosh, P. C. Young and other representatives of the G. A. R. of Columbiana Co., O., having leased for a term of years, the splendid grove near the town of Negley, known as "Camp Boquet," for the purpose of converting the same into a camping and picnic grounds, under the sole control of the G. A. R. of the County, respectfully ask you as a Post, to appoint a Committee of three to meet with us at the town of Negley, on Wednesday, October 27th, at 11 o'clock, A. M., there to elect such officers as may be necessary to manage the Association and secure its incorporation. It is proposed to make the Association profitable to the Posts that may take stock. You will please inform us whether or not you will co-operate with us in the enterprise.

By order of Committee, Yours, in F., C. & L.,
THOS. LLOYD, SEC.

East Liverpool, O., Oct. 20, 1886.

CAMP BOUQUET.

G. A. R. Re-Union

August 15th, 1889.

their membership began a steady growth. It was through their diligence that the American flag flies on public buildings today. They encouraged the singing of *America* or *The Star Spangled Banner* at public assemblies. They presented thousands of American flags to schools. Amid the social unrest of new waves of immigrants, the industrial revolution and the growing labor movements, the Grand Army of the Republic became the keeper of local tradition in the north as did their counterpart, the United Confederate Veterans, in the south.[27]

Disabled Veterans
(Courtesy Library of Congress)

It was through the Grand Army's determination that veterans' benefits first came into being.[28] In the 1880s and 1890s, the lobbying efforts of the GAR insured pensions for every veteran who had ninety days of military service. They established orphanages in seven states and soldiers' homes in sixteen states including the National Soldier's Home in Dayton, Ohio. Oftentimes, the Grand Army or its auxiliaries built these facilities then transferred them to the state to maintain and operate.

Massachusetts's Veterans' Home

Through their efforts, many battlefield sites were purchased and preserved.

The state and national organization took on greater importance as the Grand Army's role in these veteran affairs increased.

Realizing their own limitations and mortality, they founded five associated organizations: the Allied Orders of the GAR. These Allied Orders were the Sons of Veterans in 1878, the Woman's Relief Corps – their national auxiliary- in 1883, the Daughters of Union Veterans organized in 1885, but officially recognized in 1900, the Ladies of the GAR in 1886; the Auxiliary to the Sons in 1887. These are the only five organizations to receive official recognition as part of the Grand Army of the Republic family. Several other organizations were founded with similar interests, but either never sought or never received official recognition by the GAR.

In 1888, the Grand Army of the Republic held its National Encampment in Columbus, Ohio. The Naval Veterans Association, the Society of the Army of West Virginia, the Ex-Prisoners of War Association, the Sons, the Ladies, and the Relief Corps met or sent such large delegations to Columbus that it doubled the city's population for the period of the encampment.[29]

Local schools released their students to witness the Grand Parade of 68,000 former soldiers and 4,000 Sons of Veterans.

Due to the economic impact such a large influx of visitors brought, cities would actively compete for the honor of hosting the Grand Army Encampment. Badges for the Grand Army Representatives were purchased and presented by the host city to the official GAR Encampment delegates. For those attending, but not as an official delegate, numerous souvenir badges, ribbons, pins, and jewelry were available for

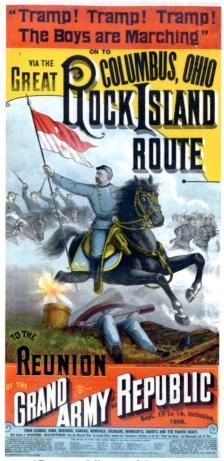

(Courtesy Library of Congress)

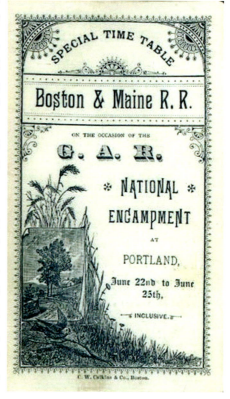

Triumphal arch erected for the 1886 San Francisco, California National Encampment
(Courtesy of Library of Congress)

purchase. Souvenirs in the form of flashed ruby glass or silver spoons were taken home to family members unable to attend a national encampment.

Many cities erected a triumphal arch over the streets through which the Grand Army and other victorious veterans marched. This parade lasted hours as tens of thousands of soldiers marched the parade route. The GAR parade had a unique feature in that it contained African-American veterans who were missing in the 1865 Grand Review in Washington, but were an important part of later Grand Army parades.

Fife and drum corps as well as singing quartets would actively compete to entertain the former soldiers. The old soldiers themselves were found entertaining each other with war stories or tall tales.[30] These events were so large the railroad companies ran special trains and offered reduced rates to those attending. Grand Army Departments often sponsored reunions at decisive battlefields such as: Gettysburg, Pennsylvania; Petersburg, Virginia; or Chattanooga, Tennessee.

Drum Corps going to Encampment
(Courtesy of Library of Congress)

In their early days while still encamped in tents a bonfire was lit and reminded the soldiers of the times spent around the evening campfire in numerous army camps. This was a time for remembrance and patriotic speeches. Years later, the patriotic program called the Grand Army Campfire remained as part of the encampment even though the encampment was held inside a hotel sans campfire.

The "boys" in blue were now reaching mid-life with families of their own. Their highest level of membership was reached in 1890 with 409,489 members organized into nearly 7,000 local posts. The requirement for membership of an honorable discharge from the Union Army sealed their fate and destiny.

In 1901, the GAR membership was 269,507.

Grand Army of the Republic National Monument (Courtesy of Library of Congress)

On July 3, 1909, the Dr. Benjamin Stephenson – Grand Army of the Republic National Monument was funded by the US House and Senate and was dedicated at Pennsylvania Ave. and Seventh Ave. in Washington, DC. It was designed by J. Massey Rhind and cost $35,000. Today it is listed on the National Register of Historic Places. In 1912, the membership was 191,346.

1915 Grand Army Encampment Parade, Washington, D.C.

 27

The Great Reunion

On July 1-4, l913, 44,713 Union veterans and 8,750 Confederate veterans gathered to commemorate the 50th anniversary of the Battle of Gettysburg.

The US Army erected 6,595 tents to house the veterans, provided 2,000 cooks to feed them and provided lighted streets, telephone and telegraph service, and emergency medical facilities.

Veterans arriving for the reunion (Courtesy of Library of Congress)

 28

As the temperature rose into triple digits, more than 700 veterans had to be treated for the excessive heat, but only nine fatalities were reported. Funding was provided by the State of Pennsylvania, other state commissions, and the federal government.

Major General Dan Sickles who had lost a leg during the battle attended. The Commanders-in-Chief of both the GAR and United Confederate Veterans spoke of the nation reunited. The veterans themselves shared war stories.

President Wilson spoke on July 4th.
(These pictures courtesy of Library of Congress)

Maj. General Dan Sickles

A great tent served as a central gathering point with 15,000 chairs.

A reenactment of Pickett's Charge on July 3 left the veterans shaking hands and weeping. A fireworks display followed.

The London (England) Telegraph is quoted: "It is impossible to spend a day in this tented city on the slopes of green pastures, where brave men fought and died so that the Republic might live, without proving that every American realizes that the North and South have trodden under their feet the bitter seeds of hate and anger and in their place have upsprung the pure flowers of friendship, esteem and affection."[31]

This event provided the first large scale service project for the newly organized Boy Scouts of America. More than 450 scouts served as escorts, greeters and provided first aid to the aging veterans. The youngest veteran attending was sixty-one and the oldest claimed to be one hundred and twelve.

"No soldier, it is said, could wander far from his comrades without one of the Scouts quickly and unostentatiously joining himself to the veteran of hard fought battles, and that without reference to whether he wore the Blue or the Gray. The withered hand was soon lain on the young shoulders, nor was it long until gray locks and boyish curls were brought close together as the tale of a vanished but never-to-be-forgotten day was poured into willing ears."[32] The relationship between the scouts and Grand Army continued at every national encampment until the early 1940s when the number of veterans decreased.

Boy Scouts providing first aid
(Pictures this page courtesy the Library of Congress)

By 1924, the membership was down to 65,382.

Although a well-established national organization, the Grand Army of the Republic operated as an Illinois state corporation until 1924. House Resolution 1869, 68th Congress 1st Session, incorporated the Grand Army of the Republic on May 19, 1924, as a federal corporation.

In 1934, the blue line of old soldiers grew much thinner with only 7,807 still enrolled.

The Next Great Reunion

A 75th anniversary commemoration of the battle of Gettysburg was held in July 1938 with 1,359 Union veterans and 486 Confederate veterans attending. The Eternal Light Peace Memorial was dedicated by President Franklin Roosevelt.

Aerial view of veterans' camp (Courtesy of National Park Service)

Secretary of War Harry Woodring welcomes UCV Commander John Claypool and GAR Commander Overton Mennet. (Courtesy of National Park Service)

Hands across the wall (Courtesy of National Park Service)

1938 Participant's Medal

200,000 gathered for the Eternal Light Peace Memorial dedication.
(Courtesy of the National Park Service)

President Franklin D. Roosevelt dedicated the monument on July 3, 1938.
(Courtesy of the National Park Service)

In 1944, the Grand Army's membership had dropped to 249 members.

 34

The Last Encampment

The Grand Army of the Republic and its Allied Orders met in Indianapolis, Indiana in September 1949 for the last time. Sixteen soldiers were listed as members of the GAR, but only six were able to attend this encampment. Old age had taken its toll. The Grand Army men aged to over 100 and disappeared one by one. The Grand Army voted that 1949 would be their final encampment. They passed resolutions that disposed of their property.

The Last Six Comrades seated left to right: Theodore Penland, Charles Chappel, Albert Woolson, Joseph Clovese, Robert Barrett, and James Hard.
(Courtesy of the Journal 1949 GAR Encampment)

While the U.S. Marine Corps band performed a concert for the encampment of the six attending veterans, Commander-in-Chief Theodore Penland, was the only one able to participate.

 Their American flag, the GAR organizational flag, the Commander-in-Chief's Colors, and their corporate seal were donated to the Smithsonian Institution and the official records and proceedings were sent to the Library of Congress. A final resolution stated as long as one member was alive, the Grand Army of the Republic was to continue.

The five organizations known as the Allied Orders of the GAR met together in one location annually until 1949.

As often happens with a death in a family, 1950 saw the Allied Orders of the GAR split apart on the national level. The Sons of Union Veterans, their Auxiliary, and the Ladies of the GAR continued meeting in one location, the Woman's Relief Corps in another, and the Daughters of Union Veterans in a third convention city. Various attempts to reunite the "family" have proven unsuccessful. On the Department (state) level, the joint meetings of all five Allied Orders have been much more successful and in many states all five do meet in the same city and on the same date. In 1954, Albert Woolson, the Senior Vice Commander-in-Chief of the GAR, created a deed of conveyance[33] naming the Sons of Union Veterans of the Civil War as the legal heir to the GAR. To honor the few remaining Union and Confederate veterans, the 84th Congress under Public Law 730, Chapter 631, dated July 18, 1956, authorized a solid gold medal weighing 10 ¼ troy ounces struck for each survivor. Albert Woolson of Duluth, Minnesota, the last member of the Grand Army of the Republic, died on August 2, 1956, at the age of 109 before his could be presented. Congress amended the bill and presented Woolson's medal to the Sons of Union Veterans who donated it to the Smithsonian Institution for display in 1957.

The medal was designed by Gilroy Roberts and produced by the US Mint. It featured U. S. Grant and Robert E. Lee on the obverse.

On the reverse: "Presented with Honor to the surviving veterans of the War Between the States Act of Congress of the United States of America." (Smithsonian Institution)

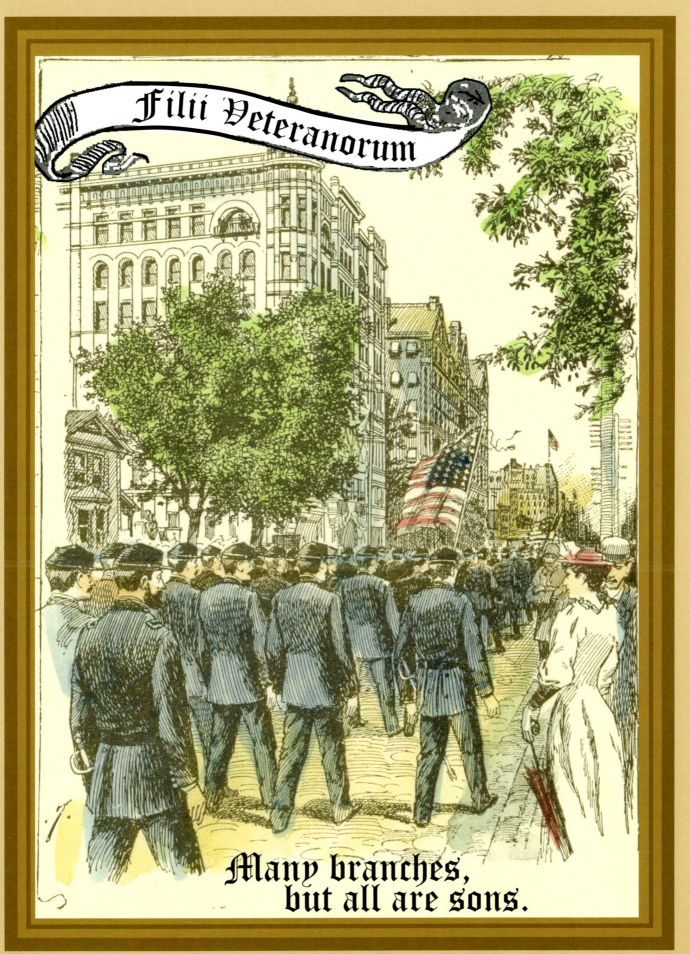

Filii Veteranorum

Many branches,
but all are sons.

Frank Leslie September 5, 1891

The Formation of the Sons of Veterans

𝔉𝔦𝔩𝔦𝔦 𝔙𝔢𝔱𝔢𝔯𝔞𝔫𝔬𝔯𝔲𝔪

Of all the Allied Orders, the Sons organization is unique in terms of history and the variety of badges produced. The Sons' fraternal structure, military training, and civilian lodge contribute to its complexity.

No one individual or region can claim to be the originator of the Sons of Veterans. The Grand Army men, realizing their own mortality, started a number of Sons organizations in the 1870s and early 1880s in eastern and western Pennsylvania, Missouri, New England, New Jersey, and New York. Three large, but separate, organizations even had similar sounding names: In Albany, New York, they were called the Filii Veteranorum (1880), Latin for Sons of Veterans. In Philadelphia, Pennsylvania they were the Cadet Corps, Sons of Veterans (1878) and in Pittsburgh, Pennsylvania they were the Sons of Veterans of Pennsylvania, but soon changed to Sons of Veterans of the United States of America (1881).

Comrade James P. Holt of Anna M. Ross GAR Post #94 of Philadelphia, Pennsylvania, made a motion on August 27, 1878, proposing a cadet corps consisting of their sons. A committee consisting of Comrades Levy W. Shengle, Carl Frederick, James P. Holt, Charles Weiss, and William Morgan was appointed by the Post. On

September 17, 1878, the post received a plan for organization and a constitution and applications were created shortly afterwards. "On September 29, 1879, the Anna M. Ross Cadet Corps #1, Sons of Veterans, was formally organized; shortly after this a cadet corps was formed in connection with Post 51, of Philadelphia. Other Posts, in this city and throughout the State of Pennsylvania, followed the example of the Posts above named in organization of the cadet corps. These junior corps were officered by members of the Grand Army of the Republic, and their principle object was the observance of Memorial Day in conjunction with their respective Posts. Lewis E. Vandergrift was the first corps captain or commander of Anna M. Ross Cadet Corps #1.

In July 1880, a Division organization was completed and Conrad Linder was elected Division Commander with the rank of Colonel, which position he held until July 1882, when James H. Classon was elected to succeed him. In the year 1881 the order spread into the states of New York, New Jersey, and Delaware; during this year a National Organization was formed and Alfred Cope was elected Commander.[34]

Edwin M. Earp, of Lynn, Massachusetts, organized the Sons of Veterans of New England and they first affiliated with the Cadet Corps headquartered in Philadelphia. In December 1884, these thirty four chapters representing more than 1,000 members became dissatisfied and merged with the Pittsburgh-based Sons.

In 1880 in Albany, New York, the GAR organized their sons into the Filii Veteranorum. This first chapter was called Frederick Townsend Post #1, Sons of Veterans. Soon numerous other posts organized throughout New York and New Jersey with a few posts in Pennsylvania.

A national organization was instituted in 1886 with John J. Dowling of Townsend Post 1 of Albany elected their first Commander-in-Chief. George W. Marks of George McClellan Post 21 of Brooklyn served as their second Commander-in-Chief.

Today, this faction is called the "Post System". The Post System believed they were perpetuating the GAR by adopting similarities to that organization. Members were greeted by the title, "comrade". The local chapter was called a "post" and their regular meetings were known as "encampments". Officers of the chapter were the Post Commander, Senior Vice Commander, Junior Vice Commander, Post Adjutant, Post Quartermaster, and Chaplain, mirroring the ranks of the GAR Post and Department.

The "Post System" ritual is strikingly similar to the GAR as well. During initiation, the recruits seeking admission received this solemn charge:

> "Whenever an enemy of liberty shall appear in our front, may the touch of elbow to elbow assure each comrade that he is supported on either side by sworn friends. Be ever ready to defend the honor of a comrade, to bind up his wounds, and to loosen the flap of your haversack to the needy. Whether quartered in the shelter tent of a private, or wearing the shoulder straps of worldly favor, remember that here all are comrades."[35]

Comrade of G.E. Smith
Post 28, SV,
Brooklyn, NY

They too produced a membership badge, lapel pin, military uniform with "SV" or "SOV" buttons, belt buckle and sword. Their badge had the flag ribbon as used on the GAR badge. Miniature rank straps were used to indicate officer's positions just as in the GAR. Stationery, calling cards, and printed literature bearing their badge were produced and are rare to find because of the eight year life of their Order.

Many Grand Army members on the national level did not approve of their Sons imitating their ritual and regalia. They felt the veterans had earned titles in battle while their Sons were "playing soldier" and wearing uniforms and insignia that rightfully should be used by the GAR alone. At the 21st GAR National Encampment held in St. Louis, Missouri on September 28-30, 1887, this resolution was proposed:

> "That we regret the action of the Sons of Veterans in some instances of calling their local Organizations "posts" and appropriating to each other the fraternal name of "Comrade" believing that these terms should remain exclusive features of the Grand Army of the Republic." [36]

The New York delegates successfully defeated this resolution, but the ill feelings between the Post System and the national GAR were clear.

The Cadet Corps organization was plagued with financial problems and could not supply badges and charters to their rapidly expanding ranks. Dissension arose and by 1886 most chapters had affiliated with the Sons of Veterans of the United States of America organization headquartered in Pittsburgh, Pennsylvania.

Clearly there were open disagreements between the various factions, with each faction vying for the Grand Army's official recognition. As early as 1881, The National Encampment of the GAR reported,

> "We also recommend to the Sons of Veterans a uniformity of name and organization, in which they shall not use the official titles of the Grand Army, and that they shall wear some prominent mark or badge or uniform to distinguish them from the Grand Army of the Republic".[37]

On April 10, 1889, the Post System Filii Veteranorum by a fifty to twenty-five vote margin merged into the Pittsburgh-based Sons of Veterans of the United States of America organization.[38] The minority held one final convention and elected as their Commander-in-Chief Joseph C. Sawyer of Matteawan, New York, on August 24, 1889, and for all practical purposes the post system had ended.[39]

Major Augustus P. Davis of Alexander Hays GAR Post # 3 of Pittsburgh, Pennsylvania, organized the Sons of Veterans of Pennsylvania in 1881. This organization quickly changed its name to Sons of Veterans of the United States of America reflecting their national expansion.[40] A ritual, bylaws, a constitution, and membership and officers badges were created.

Major Davis belonged to the GAR, the Loyal Legion, the Union Veterans League, the Union Veterans Union, the Society of the Army of the Potomac, the Society of the Army of the James, the Sons of the Revolution, the Knights of Pythias, and several Masonic Orders. He used all these connections to aid in the expansion of his Sons organization. His Order quickly spread throughout Western Pennsylvania and into Ohio and the west. He incorporated the Order in Allegheny County, Pennsylvania, and the National Organization operated under this charter for a number of years.

Major A. P. Davis

The official founding of Davis Camp #1 was November 12, 1881. The camp was named for Captain Isaac Davis, great-great grandfather of Major A. P. Davis, who fell at the Revolutionary War battle of Concord.[41] As the founding Camp of the Order, it alone was authorized to carry a flag with a solid gold background bearing the coat of arms of the Order. By the summer of 1882 a national organization had been established with Camps in thirteen states. A national encampment was called on Wednesday, October 18, 1882.

The constitution, bylaws, ritual, and insignia of Major Davis's Sons organization were approved for national use. A flag for the national organization consisting of red, white, and blue vertical stripes with the coat of arms of the Order in the center and words, "Commandery-in-Chief Sons of Veterans United States of America" was also approved.[42] Harry T. Rowley of Pittsburgh, Pennsylvania, was elected the first Commander-in-Chief. Frank Merrill, the next Commander-in-Chief, was successful in creating financial stability. The third National Encampment in 1884 was actually held in Independence Hall in Philadelphia, Pennsylvania, reflecting their political importance.

"Of the (elected) Commanders-in-Chief, three (3), Walter S. Payne, Leland J. Webb, and E. R. Campbell were soldiers and members of the Grand Army of the Republic."[43] A number of veterans were also sons of veterans and thus members of both the GAR and the Sons.

Treasurer's badge
1st National
Encampment

In order to expand the Order further, Major Davis divided the country into five Grand Divisions.[44] The First Grand Division was composed of the six New England states. The Second Grand Division was New York, New Jersey, Pennsylvania, Ohio, West Virginia, Maryland, District of Columbia, and Virginia. The Third Grand Division consisted of Illinois, Indiana, Michigan, Wisconsin, Minnesota, Iowa, Kentucky, Missouri, Kansas, Nebraska, and Dakota. The Fourth Grand Division was California, Oregon, Washington, Montana, Wyoming, Nevada, Utah, Idaho, Colorado, Arizona, and New Mexico. The Fifth and last Grand Division consisted of all the remaining Southern States.

The Grand Division Commanders were Isaac S. Bangs, Waterville, Maine; Frank Challis, New Hampshire; H. P. Kent, Massachusetts; William Ross, Baltimore, Maryland; Raphael Tobias, New York; Charles M. Catt, Columbus, Ohio; Eliot Howard Gilkey, Columbus, Ohio; William Maskell, Chicago, Illinois; Walter S. Payne, Fostoria, Ohio; R. M. J. Reed, Philadelphia, Pennsylvania; Charles S. Crysler, Missouri; Leland Webb, Topeka, Kansas; and A. V. Bohn of Leadville, Colorado.

The Grand Divisions existed from 1882 until 1885.[45] The officers of each Grand Division were Commander, Lieutenant Commander, Vice Lieutenant Commander, Adjutant General, Chief of Staff, Chief Mustering Officer, Inspector General, Medical Director, Chaplain, Ordinance Officer, Quartermaster General, and Judge Advocate General. The Divisions (State Departments) reported to these regional Grand Divisions, and the Grand Divisions reported to the national organization known as the Commandery-in-Chief.

In 1882, Grand Army of the Republic Commander-in-Chief George Merrill encouraged the expansion of the Sons of Veterans organizations, but stated the future policy of the GAR towards their allied orders: "I am opposed to opening the doors of the Grand Army of the Republic, to any person whatever, who was not himself among the defenders of the Union against rebellion. No one, not even our sons, can appreciate the memories of camp and march, of bivouac and battle, as those who were participants therein; the scenes of the great struggle can never be to them what they are to us, and while we encourage and welcome the organization of our sons in a society whose purposes are akin to ours, let our own recruiting ranks be only those closed forever with the end of the war, and when the last veteran shall receive his final discharge from life's army, let there close with him, except in its glorious record and bright memory, the last scene in the life of the Grand Army of the Republic." [46]

George Merrill

The Sons of Veterans of the United States of America soon became the dominant sons' organization. Membership, as described in the original 1882 Constitution, was based upon a complex rule of primogeniture. The First Class of membership was for the eldest son of a veteran. The Second Class was the eldest living son of a First Class member. Upon his father's death, he replaced him as a First Class member. The Third

A Vermont Brother, SV USA

Class was open to eldest sons of collateral lines, if the veteran or veteran's son had no male heirs. The Fourth Class was open to boys as young as fourteen who were named "Cadet Recruits" and could participate in the Sons of Veterans fife and drum corps.[47] They paid the muster fee and one half dues until their eighteenth birthday. Local chapters were mustered with no fewer than 15 men who were 18 years of age (sometimes, 21 years old)[48] and were known as "Camps". Their members referred to each other as "Brothers". The Camps were named, like the GAR, after deceased veterans, battles, or their location. By 1887, the rule of primogeniture was dropped as a requirement and the new eligibility read "all male descendants not less than eighteen years of age of deceased or honorably discharged soldiers, sailors, or marines, etc."[49]

Each Camp was to maintain a fife and drum corps with a bugler to provide service for parades and funerals and the position of "Camp Surgeon" was a required camp officer consisting of a medical professional who provided gratuitous medical advice and treatment to any needy member.

From 1881 until 1903, the Sons of Veterans of the United States of America was "military in its character and ceremonial work and was officered in accordance with army regulations. Camps maintained the same order and work as companies; Divisions (or state organizations) corresponded to regiments, and the Commandery-in-Chief (or national organization) to the army."

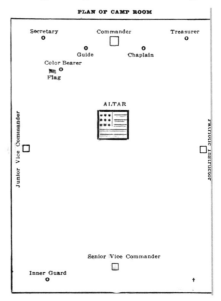

PLAN OF CAMP ROOM

Secretary o   Commander ☐   Treasurer o

o
Guide

o
Chaplain

Color Bearer
▣ o
Flag

ALTAR

Junior Vice Commander ☐   ☐ Patriotic Instructor

Senior Vice Commander ☐

Inner Guard o   †

 43

"The Captain who served as President, a First Lieutenant who served as First Vice President, and a Second Lieutenant who served as Second Vice President (were) elected by ballot. The Captain then appointed a staff consisting of an Orderly Sergeant who served as secretary, a Quartermaster-Sergeant who served as Treasurer, Chaplain, Color Sergeant, Sergeant of the Guard, Corporal of the Guard, Musician, Camp Guard, & Picket Guard."[50]

The elected Division officers were the Commander with rank of Colonel, Lieutenant Commander, Vice Lieutenant Commander, Chaplain, and three members of the Division Council. Appointed Division officers included an Adjutant, Quartermaster, Inspector, Judge Advocate, Mustering Officer, Aides-de-Camp, Sergeant Major, Quartermaster-Sergeant, and Sergeants who served as clerks to the elected officers.

Many Colonels who led Divisions commanded five to eight thousand men. Most Captains in charge of a Camp commanded 50 to 60 men.[51]

The Commandery-in-Chief elected officers consisted of the Commander-in-Chief, Lieutenant Commander-in-Chief, Vice Lieutenant Commander-in-Chief, Chief-of-Staff, Judge-Advocate-General, Chief Mustering Officer, Chaplain-in-Chief, and three members of the Council-in-Chief. The following were appointed national officers: Adjutant-General, Quartermaster-General, Assistant Inspector-Generals, and Aides-de-Camp.

In 1888 at the Twenty-Second National Encampment, Commander-in-Chief John Rea gave the Sons of Veterans of the United States of America the GAR's official recognition: "Resolved, That this Encampment endorse the objects and purposes of the Order of the Sons of Veterans, U.S.A. and hereby give to the Order the official recognition of the Grand Army of the Republic, and recommend that it aid and encourage the institution of Camps of the Sons of Veterans, U.S.A."[52]

Comdr.-in-Chief John Rea

The uniform for members [53] was to be a "dark blue flannel, single breasted sack coat, of medium length, four or five large size regulation buttons down the front, and two small regulation buttons on the under seam of each sleeve. For each three years of service, a diagonal half chevron of red silk service mark was to be sewn above these two buttons. Dark blue flannel pants,

and fatigue cap, with gold cord, embroidered or metallic wreath in front, containing "S.V." in old English silver bullion embroidery and the number of the Camp. The top of the cap may contain a device, the same to be known as the Division Badge".[54] Camps armed with military equipment could wear crossed rifles for infantry units, crossed cannons for artillery units, or crossed swords for cavalry units on the front of their caps. All commissioned officers were to wear the full dress uniform of the U.S. Army including full size shoulder straps or shoulder knots. All camps, armed or unarmed, drilled at least monthly using the U.S. Army regulations and encamped in the field. A khaki field uniform was used in some areas from the late 1890s through World War II. Most units were supplied by the United States War Department with Krag or Springfield 45-70 rifles. In some states, they were regarded as part of their state militia. Numerous military uniform articles such as hats, coats, buttons, belt buckles, and collar insignia exist with the Sons coat of arms on them. As a general rule, the "SV" and "S.O.V." buttons, buckles and swords are from the New York-based "Post System" and the coat of arms buttons, buckles and swords are from the Pittsburgh-based Sons of Veterans of the United States of America.

T.G. Carlisle
Adjutant General 1885

In 1884, a number of Grand Army men were recognized and given the rank of Past Division Commander (Colonel) or Past Grand Division Commander (Major General) and the status of Constitutional Life members. These men were: Major Augustus P. Davis, Pittsburgh, Pennsylvania; Gen. Isaac S. Bangs of Waterville, Maine; Gen. William E. W. Ross and Col. John A. Thompson of Baltimore, Maryland; Col. R. M. J. Reed of Philadelphia, Pennsylvania; Col. John Rodrigo of Newark, New Jersey; Col. William H. Pierpoint of New Haven, Connecticut; and Dr. W. S. Eldridge of Auburn, Maine. [55]

Major A. P. Davis and Col. R. M. J. Reed were bestowed with the rank of Past Commander-in- Chief.

Further research has found that others were bestowed life membership for their recruiting efforts: Carl N. Bancroft, Judge R. B. Brown, and William L. Davis of Ohio; R. M. Linton of Pennsylvania; Harold McGrew and Charles Bookwalter of Indiana; John Thurston of Nebraska; and Isaac Cutter of Illinois.

In August 1886, a merger [56] between the Philadelphia-based Sons of Veterans and the Pittsburgh-based Sons of Veterans of the United States of America occurred. As chapters were numbered in each of the organizations, Anna M. Ross Cadet Corps # 1 of Philadelphia was allowed to retain the number #1 and became Anna M. Ross Camp #1 and Davis Camp #1 was given a "star" in place of their number to show they held the position of "the charter camp". They are today and have always been referred to as Davis ★ Camp.

Similarly, nine independent chapters of the Missouri Sons of Veterans merged into the Sons of Veterans of the United States of America in 1886.

Sons of Veterans Coat of Arms

On November 20, 1888, Major Davis designed and received US design patent D 18740 for the coat of arms of the Sons of Veterans, USA. It appears on the reverse of **Type II** membership badges, on buttons, and on embossing seals. It is described as follows:

"The following instructions for painting the coat-of-arms of the Order shall be strictly adhered to: Shield - The field is white; two sabers crossed, points up, in proper colors, ensigned by a wreath of laurels, green; on a chief azure (heraldic blue cobalt); the rising sun, gold; in the disk the monogram S.V. in vermilion; on the white field. Arrange thirteen stars of five points, as in the cut, in vermilion. Supporters - On the right, a soldier in fatigue uniform (without arms) of 1861-5, viz.: dark-blue blouse, light-blue pants, Zouave cap, cross and waist belts of brown leather. On the buckle the letters U.S. On the left a sailor-navy-blue shirt and pants, black silk necktie and regulation-cap. Crest - An eagle (American) on rocks in proper colors. The scroll containing the mottos are white, shaded at the ends with crimson lake; letters black; the ornaments bordering the shield, and under the same, of gold; the flags, naval and military, with cannon and muskets, all in their proper places and colors.

Membership growth in the Sons was rapid with more than 100,000 members mustered within their first ten years, but many only served a single three year enlistment. There were just 56,000 in good standing and paying dues in 1891. [57]

Sons of Veterans , USA

By James Whitcomb Riley   July 16,1890

Sons of Veterans, USA –
Sons of soldiers passed away
Even as the smoke of war
From the land they battled for
Sons of heroes, lift your eyes
To the Old Flag in the skies
Proudly, nobly, as ye may
Sons of Veterans, USA.!

Sons of Veterans, Forget
Not the mothers mourning yet
For the gallant victors who
Marched to death and glory, too !
Through the mists of fancy see
Rank and file and panoply
The high hosts in grand array.
Sons of Veterans, USA!

Sons of Veterans, the Lord
Fashioned war of flame and sword
That your sires might wield His wrath
To smite error from His path

Lent to them His thunders too
And His lightning unto you.
Dare the old wrongs rise today
Sons of Veterans, USA !

Sons of Veterans, the might
Of brave hearts is yours by right;
By the right of house bereaved
And fortunes un-retrieved
By the right of graves unknown
Contempt by yours alone
Not their time ye can not stay
Sons of Veterans, USA !

Sons of Veterans, Behold !
Yet are blessing manifold.
Peace for you on land and sea,
Joy, content and harmony,
Souls of hope, and hearts of love,
Faith below and heaven above
So God keep us, let us pray,
Sons of Veterans, USA !

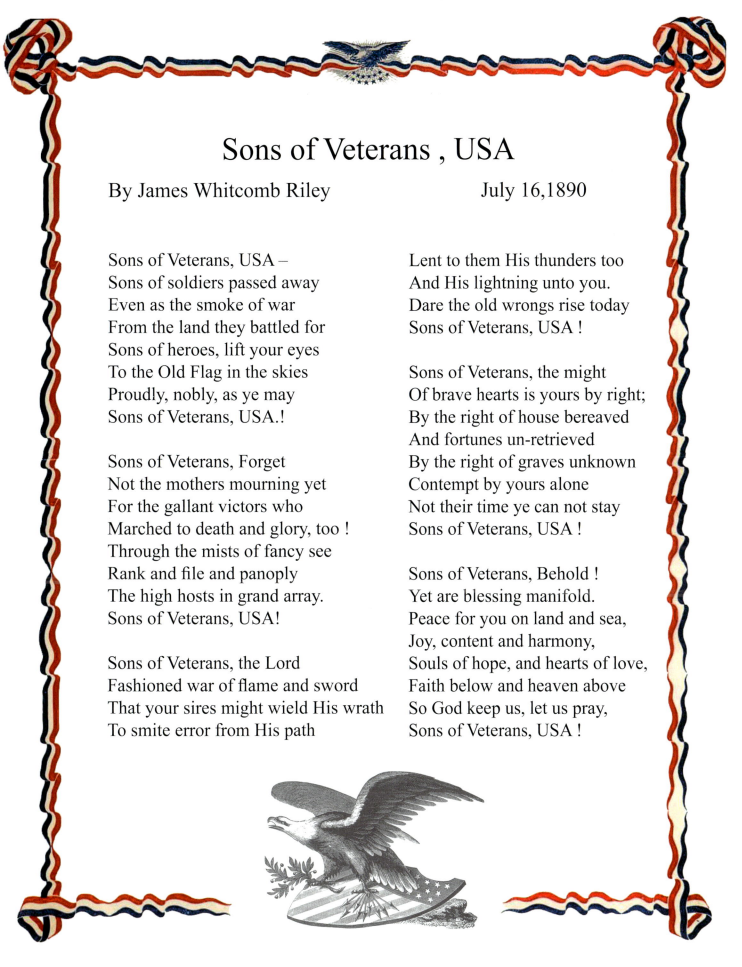

In 1894, the National Organization voted to institute a three-degree ritual.[58] Recruits would receive three separate degrees: Friendship, Loyalty, and Charity. Similar to the Grand Army's experience with multiple degrees, this Sons' experiment was short lived and a new ritual was adopted with a single degree featuring all three virtues within two years. [59]

General Benton Camp 73 of Richmond, Indiana, circa 1885
(Courtesy of Argus Ogborn)

Camps: Armed or Unarmed

While all members of the Sons of Veterans were to be uniformed, not all were armed and equipped with military weapons. The regulations of the 1880s distinguished between armed and unarmed Camps. The 1888 Sons National Encampment Proceedings reported there were four hundred and forty-one camps armed and equipped as infantry, eight as artillery, and six as cavalry.[60]

Finally, in 1891, The Sons of Veterans of the United States of America national organization established a separate "Military Rank" (department). This military department was known as the Sons of Veterans Guards.

Sons of Veterans Guards.

A company was to consist of a minimum of "21 members uniformed, armed and equipped and shall assemble for drill not less than twice each month."[61] The uniform for both armed and unarmed Camps was the same. It was to be the regulation fatigue uniform of the U.S. Army with the following changes: Buttons were to be the regulation coat of arms Sons buttons.

The cap was to have the Division cap insignia. A hat wreath contained the letters "SV" or "SVG" and was worn by all commissioned officers. Special crossed rifles, swords or cannons with the unit letter in the upper angle, and the number in the lower angle with "SV" reaching across the intersection were worn on the front of the cap by enlisted men. The sword belt buckle featured the Sons coat of arms design. The swords themselves had the coat of arms on the hilt.

SVG Member
Edward Orr of Ohio

The Commandant was appointed for one year by the Commander-in-Chief, as was an advisory committee of five Brothers. While they could be re-appointed, their term was the same as the Commander-in-Chief. Many new companies were organized in 1892.

Unfortunately, the Sons of Veterans Guards was a parallel organization to the Sons of Veterans of the United States of America. Companies and Camps competed for the same Brothers. Division Commanders and Regimental Commanders held equal rank and were often at odds. In 1893, the Sons of Veterans Guards voted independence from the Sons of Veterans, USA. At the National Encampment of the Sons of Veterans, USA in 1894, the national military department was dissolved[62] and remaining companies were placed under control of their Division Commanders again.

In 1893, the Sons of Veterans had a dues paying membership of 57,512.

Camps, armed and unarmed, held "Field Days" at the District or Division level to allow competitions in drill and marksmanship. Attendance at summer training allowed their military skills to be further improved.

Rhode Island Division
Field Day Trophy

The Sons in the Spanish-American War

This universal military training resulted in numerous Sons serving in the Spanish-American War, thus becoming veterans in their own right. They created the United Spanish War Veterans whose chapters were also known as "Camps" and the Veterans of Foreign Wars. The Sons' Commander-in-Chief Charles Darling was unable to attend the 1898 national encampment as he was leading his regiment in Puerto Rico. Commander Darling issued General Orders # 2 Series of 1898 stating: "Companies, regiments, possibly brigades, would spring from our organization throughout the land, should the call be made; *but all must be duly accepted and mustered by the constituted authorities and by them officered*... It is fully expected that our members will perform their duty, wherever the path of that duty lies, and here it is believed the matter may be safely left." [63]

SV Soldier in the Spanish-American War (Courtesy of Gary Gibson)

Camp 11 located at Manila became a company of the 10th Pennsylvania; and Camp 12 at Santa Paula, Philippines, Department of California and the Pacific, were enlisted in the 7th California.

Co. L, 33rd Michigan Infantry was made up entirely of members of the Michigan Division, Sons of Veterans USA. Michigan Camp 248 located at Augusta, Georgia, was enrolled in Co. B, 35th Michigan. Camp 59 of Princeton, Minnesota enrolled in Company M, 14th Minnesota. Pennsylvania Camp 121 at Milton formed Company C 12th Pennsylvania Infantry. Camp 269 at New Castle formed Company B of the 16th Pennsylvania. Many Kansas brothers mustered into the 20th and 21st Kansas. Many individual Sons volunteered for service in the Spanish-American War from all the states. Of the 379 US soldiers who died in the Spanish-American War, 40 were members of the Sons of Veterans USA.[64] A War Service medal was authorized to honor those veterans who were Sons members who served in combat.[65] Congress donated captured Spanish cannon to supply the bronze to manufacture it. They were hallmarked on the reverse "Sons of Veterans USA War Service" and bore an individual serial number. A numbered certificate bore the same number as the badge and was presented to the members of the Sons who saw combat in the Spanish-American War. A 115 page booklet entitled "The Roll of Honor of the Sons of Veterans, USA" was published in 1899 listing 1,967 Sons who served with honor in the Spanish-American War of 1898. It should also be noted that some camps failed to report their veterans so the exact count is unknown.

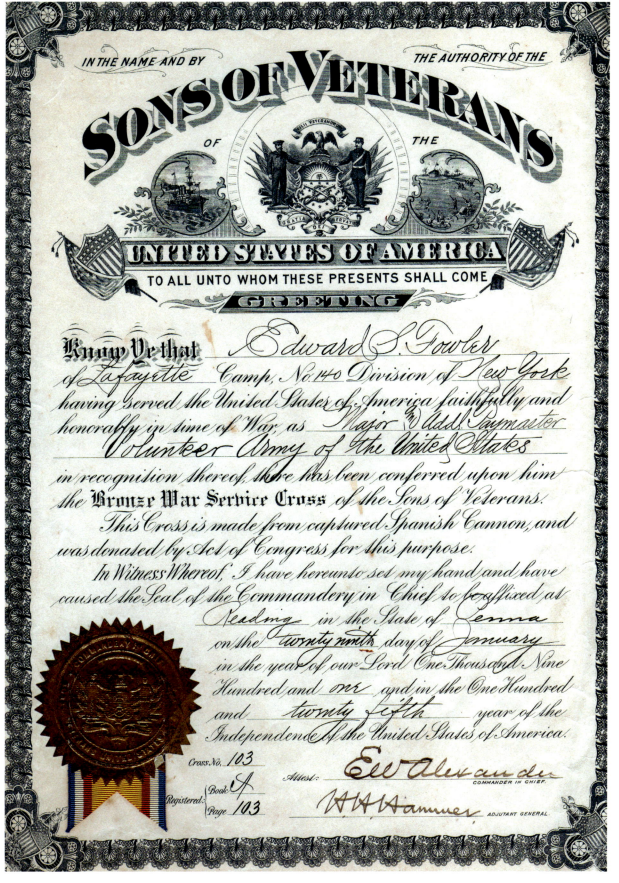

IN THE NAME AND BY   THE AUTHORITY OF THE

SONS OF VETERANS

OF   THE

UNITED STATES OF AMERICA

TO ALL UNTO WHOM THESE PRESENTS SHALL COME

GREETING

Know Ye that *Edward S. Fowler* of *Lafayette* Camp, No. *140* Division of *New York* having served the United States of America faithfully and honorably in time of War, as *Major & Add. Paymaster Volunteer Army of the United States* in recognition thereof, there has been conferred upon him the Bronze War Service Cross of the Sons of Veterans.

This Cross is made from captured Spanish Cannon, and was donated by Act of Congress for this purpose.

In Witness Whereof, I have hereunto set my hand and have caused the Seal of the Commandery in Chief to be affixed, at *Reading* in the State of *Penna* on the *twenty ninth* day of *January* in the year of our Lord One Thousand and Nine Hundred and *one* and in the One Hundred and *twenty fifth* year of the Independence of the United States of America.

Cross No. *103*

Book *A*

Registered:

Page *103*

Attest: *Edw Alexander*
COMMANDER IN CHIEF.

H. H. Hammer
ADJUTANT GENERAL.

A new century and numerous changes to the Order…

At various times, resolutions were made to admit lineal descendants of Union veterans into the Grand Army of the Republic. Every time, the old soldiers soundly defeated these resolutions. In 1904 at Boston, a GAR committee report read:

"That incorporation of members of the Order of the Sons of Veterans with membership in the Grand Army of the Republic with a view of perpetuating the name and record of our Order when those whose lives and services made that name and record possible shall have passed away, will leave the name only remaining, wholly without support in the fact of an army service membership to justify its continuance. That to admit members of the Sons of Veterans to membership in the Grand Army of the Republic upon any footing whatever is regarded as inimical to the best interest of our organization; to result in producing discord in the Post meetings; weaken the affection of the old members for the Order and hasten the day when few of the old soldiers will be found in its councils, and we are, therefore, opposed to such admission."

Similarly, resolutions on several occasions were made to change the name of the Sons of Veterans of the United States of America to the Sons of the Grand Army of the Republic.[66] Again, the Grand Army of the Republic men rejected the idea every time.

Memorial University …a tribute to the GAR

In 1900, the Sons of Veterans of the United States of America undertook their grandest project of all: the creation of Memorial University. This was a fully accredited college dedicated to the memory of the Grand Army of the Republic.[67]

 52

In 1902, the liberal arts college opened in Mason City, Iowa. A number of programs were planned including a teachers college, a business school, a music school, a military training school, and a college of oratory. One large limestone building was completed. This building housed 30 classrooms, a chapel to seat 400, and a large library.

Mason City, Iowa, was selected because it was in the center of the country with roads and rail lines making for easy access. Unfortunately, its central location was a distance from any population center. While the Iowa Department of Education accredited the college, enrollment was always low with most students on scholarships and fewer than 50 students ever graduated.

President Theodore Roosevelt was to give the dedication address. It is unknown if he did, but numerous Allied Orders members attended. Since sentiment created the Memorial University, members were asked to donate generously to its maintenance.[68] With low enrollment the financial burden became too much. In 1911, the Sons voted to close the University. There were only 75 students enrolled in the entire college and 38 were from Mason City itself.[69] The building was used until 1979 by the Mason City, Iowa, school system.[70]

Many members of the Sons of Veterans, USA themselves were now reaching mid-life and the appeal to encamp in the field and pursue military training no longer had the same attraction as it did in their youth. In 1903, the Sons of Veterans of the United States of America became a fraternal lodge with the titles of officers changing from military ranks to Commander, Senior Vice-Commander, Junior Vice-Commander, Chaplain, Secretary, Treasurer, Guard, and Guide. The office of Patriotic Instructor was added in 1906.

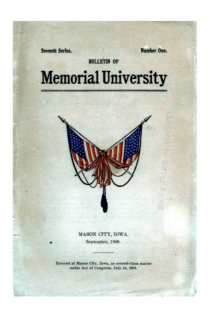

The Sons of Veterans Reserve

As the Sons of Veterans of the United States of America became a civilian lodge, they created again a military organization within themselves known as the Sons of Veterans Reserve (SVR). The Sons of Veterans Reserve were organized into brigades, regiments, battalions, and companies based upon United States Army regulations. The 1905 Constitution, Article XXIV Military Department, also called for a Sons of Veterans Naval Reserve to uniform and follow the United States Navy regulations. It is not known if any naval SVR units were ever actually organized.[71]

At various times, these units have been under the national organization's command. At other times, they have reverted to state organizational control. The commanding officer was the Sons of Veterans' National Chief of Staff. For many years, the commanding officer was Brigadier General Edwin Ames of Pennsylvania.

The Pennsylvania Brigade, SVR participated in the inauguration of President William Howard Taft in 1913.

At the tenth anniversary of the Sons of Veterans Reserve (SVR) in 1914, the SVR had 346 commissioned officers and 4,997 enlisted men.[72] The Pennsylvania Brigade was the original and largest organization within the SVR. It consisted of 197 commissioned officers and 2,960 enlisted men organized into four regiments of infantry, five troops of cavalry, two batteries of artillery, and a fully equipped field hospital unit.

Each year the SVR units encamped in the field much like the National Guard going to summer training today. Various badges are marked "Penna. Brigade• SVR". Separate encampment badges, attendance badges with service bars, and field service medals have been collected.[73] Most of these badges date from 1903 to World War I. During World War I, the First Pennsylvania Regiment SVR enlisted and was assigned to the 109th Infantry Regiment, Pennsylvania National Guard. The Fourth Pennsylvania Regiment SVR enlisted and was assigned to the 108th and 109th Machine Gun Battalions, Pennsylvania National Guard. Officially, these units were known as Pennsylvania National Guard units, but they were also SVR units. These units served as part of the Pennsylvania National Guard's famous 28th Division. A special Sons membership badge was issued to these Pennsylvania veterans who actively served in World War I.

Prior to World War I, a semi-official status continued between the Sons of Veterans Reserve and the state National Guard organizations. Senator Warren Harding of Ohio (later, U.S. President) was a member of the Sons of Veterans of the United States of America, and helped pass federal legislation equipping the SVR units with surplus military equipment. A 45-70 Springfield rifle and bayonet cost $1.50; a rifle sling $.15; a bayonet scabbard $.20; and 45-70 blank cartridges were $8.00 per thousand.[74]

Changes in federal law following World War I with regard to these semi-military organizations left the SVR as a ceremonial organization and not the military training component it had previously been.

A large number of SVR members participated in the final encampment of the Grand Army of the Republic in 1949. The Pennsylvania Brigade alone brought nearly 400 men.

Pa. Brigade Officers discuss the 1949 encampment.

 55

At the beginning of the Civil War Centennial in 1960 fewer than 300 men were enrolled in the SVR and these were under command of their various Departments usually as Camp Guards and firing squads for funerals and Memorial Day.

In order to plan for the national observance of the American Civil War Centennial, the Sons of Union Veterans once more created a National Military Department, SVR with command of all units assigned to the National Organization. The Commander-in-Chief appointed a five member advisory board known as the National Military Affairs Committee. The committee then appointed the Commanding Officer with the rank of Colonel, subject to approval by the Commander-in-Chief of the Sons. The nation was divided into three military districts: the Northern District consisting of the New England states; the Central District consisting of Pennsylvania, New York, and New Jersey; and the Western District representing Ohio, Indiana, Illinois, and any other western units. The rules and regulations of the Pennsylvania Brigade, SVR were adopted for national use. At the conclusion of the Civil War Centennial in 1965, six military districts covered all the United States with a Colonel commanding each Military District; the National Commanding Officer had the rank of Brigadier General.

1963 Gettysburg
Badge

All SVR members were required to be members in good standing of their local Sons of Union Veterans Camps. From 1961 through 1963, the "Union Forces" of most Civil War Centennial battle re-enactments were led by the SVR.

Major John Runkle
1961 Lincoln Memorial

Colonel O. G. MacPherson of Pennsylvania was the National Commanding Officer of the SVR. Conflicts in leadership led to a splintering of the SVR organization in late 1963. Twenty-eight commissioned officers and one hundred and fifty enlisted men from the Third Military District were discharged. From 1964 to 1967, a number of commemorative re-enactments were held with no official SVR presence. In 1967, many of these "re-enactment" units and individuals returned to Sons of Veterans Reserve membership. Brigadier General Chester Shriver of Gettysburg, Pennsylvania, was the national commanding officer. Major Ernest von Frankenberg of Milwaukee, Wisconsin, later promoted to Lieutenant Colonel, was Deputy Commander. Major Robert J. Wolz, the author of this book, served as The Quartermaster General, SVR and later, as The Adjutant General, SVR. He proposed with Brother William Orr of Youngstown, Ohio, the first National SVR Encampment held at Lisbon, Ohio, in July, 1970. These annual National SVR Encampments continued into the early 1990s. These were large gatherings of Civil War uniformed soldiers who "re-enacted" a battle for the public. Other activities included a "Grand Parade" of troops and a Civil War style military ball. Life-long friendships were formed around campfires in the evening hours and in large part, the whole family was involved in this living history activity. An amazing

Chet Shriver and R.C. Wolz at 1971 National Encampment.

safety record exists as fewer than a dozen serious accidents occurred from 1960 through the 1980s with thousands of troops, Union and Confederate, firing tons of black powder blanks in rifles and cannons.

Of course, the SVR since its beginning has participated in the National Encampments of the GAR and the Sons in the form of escorts, honor guards, and color bearers for the GAR Campfire program and in all the national programs like Lincoln's Birthday, Lincoln's Death Day, Remembrance Day, and of course, Memorial Day.

SVR Calvary 1967

The federal blue uniforms of the Sons of Veterans Reserve remains the visual link between today's Sons of Union Veterans and the Civil War veterans of the Grand Army of the Republic.

The Junior Order Sons of Veterans, USA [75]

In 1908 in Framingham, Massachusetts, the Sons wanted to attract more grandsons into the Order. Camp # 1 of the Junior Order, Sons of Veterans, USA, was organized for boys between the age of 12 and 18. A constitution, bylaws and ritual were developed. A Junior Camp consisted of fifteen boys under the direction of a senior camp. Elections were held every June and December. The Junior Camps could choose their own uniform. One suggestion was white trousers with dark blue shirts. In some cities, the Junior Camps grew large and upon reaching the age of 18 the members transferred into regular membership. The Junior Order quietly faded from existence by 1924. The 1918 Sons' proceedings reported a national membership of eighteen junior camps and five hundred and fifty-nine junior members. In 1949 through 1953, an unsuccessful attempt was made to revive the Junior Order.

GAR Band Canton,Ohio
(Courtesy of the Library of Congress)

The Sons of Veterans March

In late Victorian times, most cities in America had military styled bands that entertained the citizens with concerts on the village green. Canton, Ohio, had a number of local musicians that formed two exceptional fine bands: The Thayer Military Band and the Grand Army Band. Karl Lawrence King played in both.

On June 23, 1909, Karl Lawrence King copyrighted *The Sons of Veterans March*. This march was composed when King was 18 years of age and is one of his first published works. He wrote more than 200 marches and shares the title of March King with John Philip Sousa. The *Sons of Veterans March* has parts for flute, piccolo, oboe, bassoon, clarinet, saxophone, cornet, F horn, trombone, euphonium, tuba, snare, bass drums, and cymbals. While rarely heard by members of the Sons, it remains a popular march in high school and college band competitions. A recent (2013) search on Youtube.com found several renditions by various bands.

The Sons Of Veterans Reserve March

In 1933, Captain C. LeRoy Stoudt of the Pennsylvania Brigade, Sons of Veterans Reserve wrote the *SVR March* dedicated to the Sons and the GAR. It is a much simpler musical tribute than the *Sons of Veterans March* described above, with music by Fred Cardin and words by LeRoy Stoudt who later served as Commander-in-Chief of the Sons in 1943.

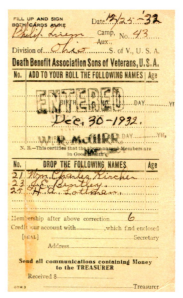

The Death Benefits Association

Life insurance prior to World War II was a luxury of the rich and many organizations created mutual life insurance companies to attract and retain members. The Masonic Orders, Odd Fellows, Knights of Maccabees, Knights of Columbus, and most other large fraternities had already offered insurance benefits to their members. So for several years and in numerous pages of proceedings the debate raged if the Sons of Veterans of the United States of America could offer its members insurance. State laws were enacted to protect individuals from fraud on the part of these lodges and to ensure that if premiums were paid benefits would also be paid.

As an alternative to a full scale insurance company, the Sons of Veterans and its auxiliary organized a "death benefits association" in 1893 within its membership to provide some form of insurance for members or their spouses.[76] A monthly premium of twenty cents was sent into the death benefit association. At the time of a death, a subscriber's family would receive $100 to $250 in death benefits, if the member had paid membership dues to the Sons or Auxiliary and had been a subscriber for a year or longer. In the year 1914, the Commander-in-Chief reported $22,000 in benefits had been paid out the previous year.[77] These death benefit societies fell from favor as life insurance became more readily available to the masses. The Sons Death Benefit Society officially closed in 1971 with PDC Clarence Riddell of Pennsylvania serving as their last treasurer.

On August 1, 1910, a camp was organized under the Department of Pennsylvania in Buenos Aires, Argentina. Likewise, in 1915, the New York Department chartered a camp on the Iroquois reservation in western New York.

In 1917, the Sons membership stood at 57,824 dues paying members.

Multiple generations of the Manning Family of Philadelphia. Pa.

Another War and More Veterans

During World War I, numerous grandsons of Union Veterans went off to war. The Sons of Veterans with its auxiliary collected $26,426.65 for fourteen ambulances to be sent overseas.[78] Many of these returning veterans helped form the American Legion at the close of the war and thus their own veterans' organization.

As the Grand Army's ranks were quickly thinning, the Sons of Veterans members were allowed to serve as Post, and later Department, Secretaries for the GAR. This position was always extended without voice and without vote in the Post or Department. Katherine Flood and later Cora Gillis, both Past National Presidents of the Daughters of Union Veterans, each served a number of years as the GAR's National Secretary. Today, based upon the scope of duties, we would probably call this national secretary an executive director for the GAR.

Cora Gillis

In 1920, the Sons of Veterans had 51,130 dues paying members.

Clara Barton Camp, Richmond, Virginia, May 30, 1917
Descendants of U.S. Colored Troops

Black and White Camps

In most cases, the Sons followed the example of the Grand Army with regard to race relations allowing African-Americans and other minorities into their camps, but there were numerous segregated camps especially in the old South. A remnant still existed in the early 1960s with all black camps in Beaufort, South Carolina; Paris, Kentucky; and Wilmington, Delaware. The Wilmington Camp, in fact, operated the Sons of Veterans Library Association to fund their programs having obtained a liquor license under their charter much as American Legion or Veterans of Foreign Wars Posts often do.

A New Name for the Sons of Veterans, USA

The confusion caused by their name, Sons of Veterans, USA, continued with children of the Spanish-American War and World War I veterans wanting to join.

In 1922, three different names were proposed by the GAR National Encampment for the Sons. These were Sons of Union Veterans of the Civil War, Sons of Union Veterans of the War of 1861-1865, and Sons of Defenders of the Union. Some Sons Departments continued to press for the name, Sons of the Grand Army of the Republic.

In 1923, the Sons of Veterans of the United States of America national encampment adopted:

> "...a resolution asking the National Encampment of the Grand Army of the Republic to name a committee representing that Organization to confer with a committee to be named to represent the Order of the Sons of Veterans, USA, to consider among other things, a change in the name of the Order of Sons of Veterans that would more clearly indicate and designate of whom the Order consists."[79]

The joint GAR and Sons committee reported 'the Sons of the GAR' was preferable, but GAR Headquarters issued General Orders # 6 stating, "The name hereafter to be borne by the Sons of Veterans is not yet settled and may be determined at the (1924) Boston encampment." The GAR attempted to influence a merger of all the women's organizations into a single organization at the Boston encampment, but no name was selected for the Sons.

The Grand Army of the Republic's 59th National Encampment held in Grand Rapids on September 3, 1925 officially approved the name change to Sons of Union Veterans of the Civil War. A resolution was adopted by the Sons "to take such legal action as may be necessary to cause the corporate name of the Order of Sons of Veterans United States of America to be changed to that of "Sons of Union Veterans of the Civil War".[80]

President Calvin Coolidge and Sons
Comdr-in-Chief Bill Coffin
(Courtesy Library of Congress)

Similarly, the Daughters of Veterans and Sons of Veterans Auxiliary also changed their names on September 3, 1925.

In 1928, the National Encampment of the GAR authorized the Sons of Veterans to assume the Grand Army's place in conducting Memorial Day Services. This was a response by the GAR to younger veterans' organizations attempts to usurp the GAR's position as head of Memorial Day services. The Great Depression took its toll on most organizations as unemployed men and families could not afford the luxury of paying dues. In 1934, the Sons of Union Veterans membership stood at 28,618.

Central Region
(Gary Gibson)

In 1935, the Sons of Union Veterans National Encampment passed a resolution creating four regional organizations of Sons and Auxiliary for the purpose of encouraging fellowship. These were the New England Region, the Eastern Region, the Central Region, and the Western Region. The format usually included a speaker and a dinner meeting. Some regions later added round table discussion groups to their dinner meeting. The presidency usually rotated between a member of the Sons and a member of the Auxiliary. In 2013, only the New England Region and Central Region are still meeting.

New England
Region

The GAR Highway

Beginning in 1934, the Sons again sought recognition for the Grand Army by naming US Route 6 as the GAR Highway beginning in Provincetown, Massachusetts and ending at Long Beach, California. The following quotes the Federal Highway Administration:

"Major William L. Anderson, Jr., of the U.S. Army conceived the idea of designating U.S. 6 the Grand Army of the Republic Highway to honor the Union forces during the Civil War. Based on his recommendation, the Sons of Union Veterans of the Civil War began promoting the idea in April 1934. Because the highway was owned by the States, the organization asked each State to act on the proposal. The first to do so was Massachusetts when Governor Charles F. Hurley signed a bill on February 12, 1937, naming the route. Over the years, the States gradually adopted the name. For example, California did so in 1943 and Indiana in 1946, while Governor James Duff of Pennsylvania named the State's segment of U.S. 6 in 1948.

(Courtesy of
Jerry Orton)

 63

"A formal dedication of the Grand Army of the Republic Highway took place on May 3, 1953, in Long Beach, California. The occasion was a gathering of the five (Allied GAR) organizations…. The five organizations held their own meetings, but came together for the dedication on that Sunday afternoon to place a monument in front of the Municipal Auditorium:

GRAND ARMY OF THE REPUBLIC HIGHWAY

U.S. ROUTE 6

"'This monument marks the western end of a coast to coast highway extending a distance of three thousand six hundred fifty-two miles through fourteen states. It was erected by the Sons of Union Veterans of the Civil War in memory of the heroic services and unselfish devotion of the Union soldiers, sailors, and marines who laid down their lives on the altar of sacrifice during the Civil War. (The) National Highway (was) first proposed by Major William L. Anderson, Jr., U.S.A. of Massachusetts. For what they did and dared, let us remember them today.'"[81]

Signs designating the highway were erected in all fourteen states. Sadly, due to budget considerations only a few signs remain in some states in 2014.

The years of World War II and the Korean Conflict saw grandsons and great-grandsons of Civil War veterans once more answer freedom's call and return to form yet more veteran orders. Whereas in the 1890s there was only one organization for young men to join, now there are a dozen organizations based upon their own military service. In 1953, Sons of Union Veterans membership stood at 8,863. In 1953, the National Encampment first authorized Associates for those men interested in the Order but lacking blood kinship to a Union veteran.

In its early years, the Sons of Veterans of the United States of America operated under its Allegheny County, Pennsylvania incorporation. In 1888, they became incorporated in the State of Illinois. In 1911, they considered seeking a federal charter, but decided to wait and learn from the GAR's effort to obtain a federal charter. The GAR federal incorporation occurred in 1924. However the Sons continued to operate under their Illinois incorporation until 1954.

In 1954, the Sons of Union Veterans of the Civil War became a federally chartered organization by act of Congress under Public Law #605 enacted on August 20, 1954. Notable among the incorporators were General Douglas MacArthur, Major General Amos Fries, and Major General U. S. Grant III.

The Sons bestowed Honorary Membership on several members of Congress for their help in the incorporation: Senator Everett Dirkson (R-Ill), Senator Kenneth Keating (R-NY), Representative George Dondero (R-MI) and Representative William J. B. Dorn (D-SC).

With the passing of the Grand Army, the Sons created several new programs while maintaining their involvement in older observances.

The Grand Army Remembrance Day program began in 1956 and continues each November in commemoration of President Lincoln's Gettysburg Address.

Each April the Sons are joined with the Loyal Legion at Lincoln's Tomb in Springfield, Illinois, in commemoration of Lincoln's Death.

Chester Shriver at
1956 Remembrance Day

1972 Lincoln Memorial. Standing L to R
Bill Greene, Wilbur Haueter, Bob Wolz, Bob Davis

The Sons continue their observance of Lincoln's Birthday each February 12 as guests of the Loyal Legion.

Memorial Day is observed each May in numerous communities as well as at the Arlington National Cemetery; the Cathedral of the Pines in Rindge, New Hampshire; and at the Gettysburg National Battlefield Park.

The United States Code was revised in 1998 and an updated Federal Charter was granted under Title 36 US Code – Patriotic and National Observances, Ceremonies and Organizations – Chapter 2003, The Sons of Union Veterans of the Civil War.

In February 1954, Senior Vice Commander-in-Chief Albert Woolson, the last surviving member of the GAR, signed a deed of conveyance transferring all Grand

Army property not already disposed of to the Sons of Union Veterans. In 1956, upon the death of Comrade Woolson, the Sons of Union Veterans of the Civil War became the legal heir of the Grand Army of the Republic.

General U. S. Grant III, a Son's Past Commander-in-Chief, was named to lead the United States Civil War Centennial Commission in 1958.

The Civil War Centennial brought some renewed interest to the Sons of Union Veterans organization and a number of young men came into our ranks, but the American Revolution bicentennial soon came to the forefront and some of these living history enthusiasts moved on to the bicentennial events and left the Sons.

Front: Gen. U.S. Grant III, SUVCW and
Col. John May, SCV
Rear: Col. LeRoy Stoudt and
Dr. W.W. Stevens
(Courtesy of LeRoy Stoudt)

The 1970s saw the Sons reach a low point in membership as American society underwent a number of changes. Some assumed the Allied Orders had gone out of existence with the Grand Army of the Republic. Some were anti-military as an aftermath of the Vietnam War, and finally, to many, all fraternities and lodges seemed passé. Men were working multiple jobs or simply came home to watch television and were unwilling to join anything. Men's and women's lodges were simply a relic of the Gilded Age, a distant memory of the past for many.

The Sons of Union Veterans membership in 1978 stood at 2,560.

The 1980s and early 1990s has brought forth a new wave of membership inquiries. Television series, like *The Blue and the Grey* and Ken Burns's *The Civil War*, brought renewed interest in the American Civil War. Genealogy has grown as a popular pastime and the internet has allowed hundreds of thousands to "discover" their roots and for many their eligibility to one of the Allied GAR Orders.

In 2002, the Sons membership stood at 6,350 members in twenty-six Departments.

In March 2003, a group of Sons established the Sons of Union Veterans Charitable Foundation, recognized as a 501(c)(3) organization by the Internal Revenue Service, they have raised and collected money in order to provide grants primarily for monument restoration. There are three levels of Lincoln Fellows and three levels of Sentinels among their contributors. This program is strictly voluntary.

For more information about the Sons or any of the Allied GAR Orders, details can be found on the World Wide Web: http://www.suvcw.org

Today with increasing membership and financial strength, the Sons have active committees focused on Civil War grave registration and preserving Civil War monuments, historic sites, and artifacts. They are aggressively guarding memorials and hold them as a public trust for future generations to enjoy. They annually award two college scholarships.

In 2001, Sons Commander-in-Chief Edward Krieser summed up the new attitude of the organization:

"We have a duty to continue to preserve and perpetuate the memory of our Fathers who saw their duty and performed their duty to the best of their ability. We, as their heirs can do no less."[82]

On the eve of the Civil War Sesquicentennial in 2011, there were 6,441 dues paying members in the Sons in twenty-six departments.

President Warren Harding with Maryland Delegation, July 30, 1923.
Front Row: Ardin Carrick, Rep. James Glynn, S.M. Croft, Clinton Hiatt, H.V. Speelman*, President Warren Harding, Frank DeCroft, Rep. Clifford Ireland*, E.F. Warneer, James Lyons, S.A. Smith, and F. Johnson.
Back Row: Dr. A. Taylor, Rep AEB Stephens*, William Coffin*, and Rep. Everett Sanders.
(*Sons Comander-in-Chief)

Of The

Military Order

Loyal Legion

Kindred Societies to the GAR

The Military Order of the Loyal Legion of the United States

On April 15, 1865, a group of Union officers gathered in Philadelphia, Pennsylvania, their purpose centered on forming an Honor Guard for President Lincoln's funeral and perhaps come to the aid of their country if the assassination was a Confederate plot.

The former officers wore "a badge of crepe upon the left arm for a period of thirty days, as a token of respect for (the) deceased Commander-in-Chief. When attending the President's funeral they were to wear black clothes…, fatigue caps, crepe on the left arm. National Colors in the left button-hole and white gloves."[83]

A notice in the Philadelphia newspapers makes the first reference to the Loyal Legion on May 11, 1865:

"A meeting of the Military Order of the Loyal Legion of the United States will be held at the county courthouse, Sixth and Chestnut Streets, on Wednesday evening May 31, 1865, at eight o'clock. All officers and ex-officers of the army, navy, and marine corps interested in the establishment of an organization founded to perpetuate the memories and associations of the present war are invited to attend. Signed, by order, Sam B. Wylie Mitchell, Secretary."[84]

Lt. Col. Thomas E. Zell   Lt. Col. Samuel B. W. Mitchell   Capt. Peter Keyser

Lieutenant Colonel Thomas Ellwood Zell, Third Battery, Pennsylvania Infantry; Lieutenant Colonel Samuel B. W. Mitchell, surgeon, Eighth Pennsylvania Cavalry; and Captain Peter Keyser of the Ninety-First Pennsylvania are considered the founders of the Military Order of the Loyal Legion of the United States.

Several meetings occurred over the summer and a permanent organization known as the Commandery of the State of Pennsylvania, Military Order of the Loyal Legion of the United States was organized on November 4, 1865.

These tenets and objects were the basis of the organization:

"First. A firm belief and trust in Almighty God.

"Second. True allegiance to the United States of America, based upon paramount respect for, and fidelity to, the National Constitutions and Laws.

"The objects of this Order shall be to cherish the memories and associations of the war waged in defense of the unity and indivisibility of the Republic; strengthen the ties of fraternal fellowship and sympathy formed by companionship-in-arms; advance the best interests of the soldiers and sailors of the United States, especially those associated as Companions of this Order, and extend all possible relief to their widows and children; foster the cultivation of military and naval science; enforce unqualified allegiance to the General Government; protect the rights and liberties of American Citizenship, and maintain National Honor, Union and Independence."

The Coat of Arms, badge, seal, and mottos were designed by Colonel Samuel B. W. Mitchell. The Loyal Legion is incorporated in Pennsylvania.

Major General George Cadwalader was elected Commander and Colonel Samuel B. W. Mitchell served as Recorder. As this was the founding state they served as Acting Commander-in-Chief and Recorder-in-Chief. Major General Winfield Scott Hancock was elected the next Commander-in-Chief and John P. Nicholson assumed the position of Recorder-in-Chief.

General Cadwalader (Courtesy Mass. MOLLUS)

Mr. Nicholson was perhaps the single person who should be credited with the expansion of the Loyal Legion. He was well known in numerous veteran circles and used his influence for the betterment of the Loyal Legion; he devoted his free time to the organization, collecting dues and records. Mr. Nicholson had one of the largest personal literary collections on the Civil War (17,000 books) which he donated to the Loyal Legion's War Library. Mr. Nicholson served as chairman of the Gettysburg Military Park Commission and president of the Valley Forge Park Commission; he remained in the position of Recorder-in-Chief until his death in 1922.

On October 21, 1885, the organization expanded to a national basis.

Ely Samuel Parker, Sachem of the Seneca tribe of New York, was elected into membership in 1887. He had served as General U. S. Grant's military secretary and wrote the official documents that ended the war at Appomattox Court House, Virginia.

In 1892, the Loyal Legion had 20 state commanderies with 6,323 First Class (veteran) companions, 329 Second Class companions (hereditary), and 93 Third Class or Gentlemen companions.[86]

Unlike the Grand Army, The Loyal Legion had three types of membership from its beginning. The first was based upon the veteran holding a commission and serving in Federal forces prior to April 15, 1865. These were designated as Original Companions of the First Class. The second were Hereditary Companions who would replace their fathers under the rules of primogeniture as the Original Companions died. A third class or honorary class was open to "gentlemen" who distinguished themselves with conspicuous support of the Union (usually state and federal politicians) and who were elected into membership prior to April 15, 1890.[87] All members were 21 years of age and called "Companions".

Original Companions of the First Class (the veterans) consisted of nearly all the prominent Union officers beginning with Generals Ulysses S. Grant, William T. Sherman, Philip H. Sheridan, Nelson A. Miles, John M. Schofield, Winfield Scott Hancock, George B. McClellan, Rutherford B. Hayes, George Armstrong Custer, David McMurtrie Gregg, and Grenville M. Dodge; Admirals David G. Farragut, Bancroft Gherardi, and George W. Melville.

Five original veteran Companions (U. S. Grant, Rutherford B. Hayes, Chester A. Arthur, Benjamin Harrison, and William McKinley) served as Presidents of the United States, as did three Honorary Companions: Herbert Hoover, William Howard Taft, and Dwight David Eisenhower.

Original honorary members included Vice President Hannibal Hamlin, Secretary of State William Seward, Secretary of War Edwin Stanton, Secretary of the Navy Gideon Welles, and Secretary of the Treasury Salmon Chase, also by special resolution posthumously, President Abraham Lincoln.

All legislative power rests in the national convention called a Congress. Originally these were held every four years in April. Today they meet annually with a mid-year meeting in February and the Congress in October. Voting representatives include elected Commandery-in-Chief officers, State Commanders, past commanders-in-chief, past state commanders, vice commanders, past vice commanders, recorders, and past recorders of the various state commanderies.

As the number of hereditary members grew, the veteran companions alone were eligible to elect other veterans into membership, but all companions would elect hereditary members.

Today, membership exists in four classes. Hereditary membership is open to all lineal or collateral male descendants 18 years of age or older. Junior membership is open to all lineal or collateral male descendants under the age of 18. Associates were created on July 1, 1989, and open to those who lack descent from a commissioned officer, but are interested in the purposes of the society. This Honorary membership is bestowed by the Commandery-in-Chief. The national organization is known as the Commandery-in-Chief. Regional organizations were originally referred to as "Grand Commanderies" and are today called "State Commanderies" and local chapters were called "District Commanderies". No District Commanderies exist today. Each level had the following officers: a Commander, Senior Vice Commander, Junior Vice Commander, a Recorder who served as Secretary, a Registrar responsible for membership records, a Chaplain, and a five-member executive board known as the Board of Officers.

In 1915, on their 50th anniversary, there were 7,663 members. Of these 3,550 were veteran companions and the balance hereditary members.

General Douglas MacArthur, Major General U. S. Grant III and Vice President Charles Dawes were hereditary members, as were Fleet Admiral Chester Nimitz, General Omar Bradley, and Henry Stimson (Secretary of State under Hoover and Secretary of War under Presidents Roosevelt and Truman).

We are forever indebted for the foresight shown by these early companions in the preservation of Civil War history.

Ranking high on the list of Loyal Legion activities were regular banquets with the principal speaker presenting his recollections of a Civil War event or battle. These speeches were then published between 1887 and 1915 in a series of books and pamphlets called the *War Papers* and provide an important primary resource for Civil War researchers today. In 1992, Broadfoot Publishing Company reprinted the series of 70 volumes of *War Papers*.

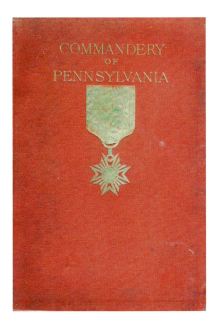 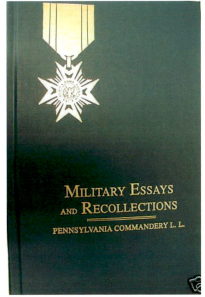 

These are examples of the original War Papers.

Like the GAR, frequent reunions were held with visits to the decisive battlefields… Gettysburg being a favorite.

In 1884, dedication of the Cavalry Monument at Gettysburg occurred. Captain Peter Keyser, a founder of Mollus, is shown in the center with his Legion badge proudly worn. (Photo courtesy of Mass. MOLLUS / US ARMY History Center)

In April 1890, the Massachusetts Commandery held a week long reunion in Gettysburg as witnessed in these photographs.

Top: Mass. Commandery at Gettysburg

At Left: Bugler Henry on
          Little Round Top 1890

Bottom: Pennsylvania Commandery
          Oct 5, 1893, at Gettysburg.

(Photos courtesy of MOLLUS / US
          Army History Center)

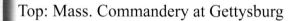

The Washington, DC Commandery was instrumental in urging the US government's printing of the "The War of Rebellion: A Compilation of the Official Records of the Union and Confederate Armies."

The Massachusetts Commandery chose to acquire and preserve the photographic plates of Matthew Brady, Alexander Gardner, and Samuel Cooley. These have recently been donated to the U.S. Army History Center at Carlisle, Pennsylvania.

In 1888, they collected arms and armament donated by the Companions and these artifacts became the basis for the MOLLUS War Library and Museum.

(Photos courtesy of MOLLUS / US Army History Center)

Delegates gather for 1904 National Congress at Portland, Maine.
(Courtesy of MOLLUS/US Army History Center)

Lincoln Memorial in Washington, DC

In 1910, the US Congress appointed the Lincoln Memorial Commission with funding to build the monument to our 16th president. Former President William Howard Taft was named the Commission's Chairman. On Memorial Day, May 30, 1922, Chairman Taft presented the Lincoln Memorial to President Warren G. Harding who received it on behalf of the American people. The dedication ceremony was under the auspices of the Military Order of the Loyal Legion. Seventy-nine year old Robert Todd Lincoln attended. Each year since, the Loyal Legion and Sons of Union Veterans have participated in Lincoln Birthday wreath laying on February 12. In 2009, the Loyal Legion rededicated the Lincoln Memorial as part of the Abraham Lincoln bicentennial. The Lincoln Memorial remains the most visited monument in Washington, DC. (Construction photos courtesy of Library of Congress.)

William Howard Taft, Commission Chairman, President Warren Harding,
and Robert Todd Lincoln   (Courtesy of Library of Congress)

Companions of the Washington D.C. Commandery circa 1925
(Courtesy of Library of Congress)

 77

Maryland Department Sons and Auxiliary Feb 1925 (Courtesy of Library of Congress)

Gen. U. S. Grant III participates at
Lincoln Memorial Feb. 12, 1948.
(National Archives / Truman Library)

President Eisenhower participates at Lincoln
Memorial Feb. 12, 1954.
(National Park Service / Eisenhower Library)

On July 1, 1989, Dr. Ernesto Ego-Aguirre of New York was elected as the first Associate Companion.

The Loyal Legion museum collection and war library was headquartered at 1805 Pine Street in Philadelphia. The Companions were aware they lacked the space needed and the professional staff to care for this collection of more than 20,000 objects that had been donated by original companions. In 2003, an independent board of directors was created to seek grants and try to broaden the museum's appeal by changing its name to the Civil War Library and Underground Railroad Museum. A lack of funding prevented the opening of this museum and much of the collection remained in storage independent of its Loyal Legion roots.

In 2011, a small part of the Loyal Legion's collection was loaned to the Gettysburg National Military Park and it is hoped that the new Civil War Museum of Philadelphia may open in 2014, finally allowing the greatest collection of Civil War artifacts outside of the federal government to be displayed.

In 2010, there were 863 companions enrolled in 19 state commandries.

For information on membership, details can be found on the World Wide Web at http://www.suvcw.org/mollus/mollus.htm

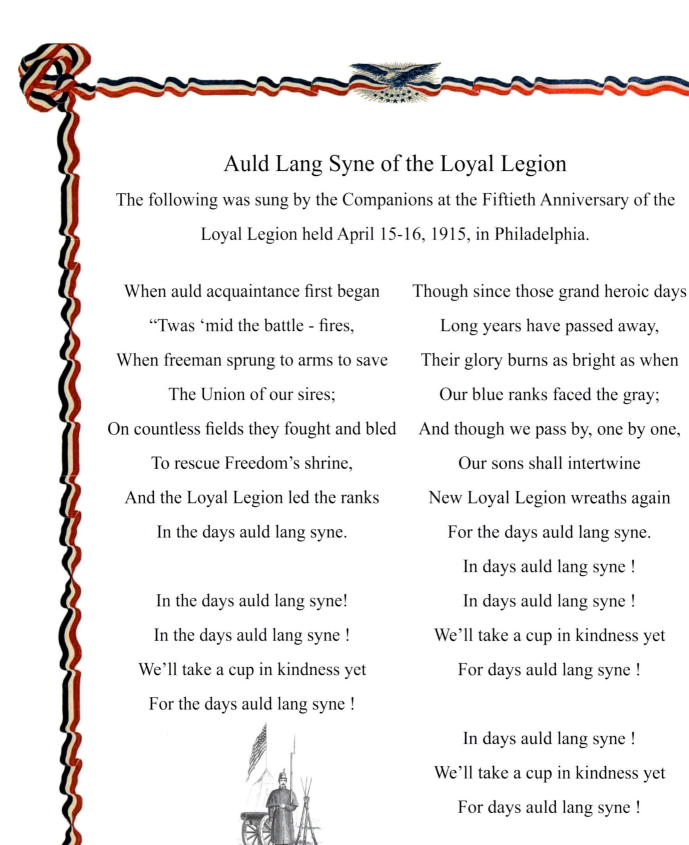

Auld Lang Syne of the Loyal Legion

The following was sung by the Companions at the Fiftieth Anniversary of the
Loyal Legion held April 15-16, 1915, in Philadelphia.

When auld acquaintance first began
"Twas 'mid the battle - fires,
When freeman sprung to arms to save
The Union of our sires;
On countless fields they fought and bled
To rescue Freedom's shrine,
And the Loyal Legion led the ranks
In the days auld lang syne.

In the days auld lang syne!
In the days auld lang syne !
We'll take a cup in kindness yet
For the days auld lang syne !

Though since those grand heroic days
Long years have passed away,
Their glory burns as bright as when
Our blue ranks faced the gray;
And though we pass by, one by one,
Our sons shall intertwine
New Loyal Legion wreaths again
For the days auld lang syne.

In days auld lang syne !
In days auld lang syne !
We'll take a cup in kindness yet
For days auld lang syne !

In days auld lang syne !
We'll take a cup in kindness yet
For days auld lang syne !

Splinter Organizations

Sons of the Grand Army of the Republic

As previously mentioned, Grand Army Posts considered organizing their sons into a formal organization at various times. One membership badge marked "S. of GAR 1870" has been located. This would be one of the earliest efforts documented thus far as that is only four years after the GAR itself organized. No printed materials or records have been found about this order nor do we even know where it may have started, but the lack of information would indicate it was very short lived and unsuccessful so Anna Ross Camp # 1 in Philadelphia can still claim to be the first successful attempt to organize Grand Army sons.

On several occasions, some members of the Sons of Veterans felt they would be better recognized if their organization was known as the Sons of the GAR. The National Encampments of the GAR and the Sons of Veterans, USA, rejected these resolutions from the various Camps and Departments. Pennsylvania Sons Past Department Commander William Kearney was inducted into one of these splinter groups around 1910 and wore his "Sons of the GAR" membership badge. No badge image for this order has been located for this book. Their effort was short-lived and they returned to the Sons of Veterans of the United States of America.

In 1934, the National Daughters of the GAR, Inc. demanded recognition by the GAR and the other Allied Orders and threatened to organize the National Sons of the GAR, Inc. if GAR recognition was not forthcoming. It was an unsuccessful threat; they did not receive recognition as an Allied Order and the National Sons of the GAR did not occur.

Children of the Grand Army of the Republic

The National Daughters of the Grand Army of the Republic, Inc. organized their sons and daughters into a junior order. This Junior Order was named the Children of the GAR, organized in Detroit, Michigan, in March 1914 for girls and boys ages 5 to 16.

The Junior Order had chapters called "Pickets" under the guidance of a Daughters of the GAR chapter known as a "Fortress". The Junior Order's membership pin was described in their regulations as a triangle that said "Children" across the top with "of the" and "GAR' on the two sides. The center features the GAR soldier and sailor from the GAR badge obverse. No example of this pin has been located.

The Daughters of the GAR was a regional organization located in Illinois, Michigan, and Wisconsin and never grew to national strength so the Children of the GAR too must have been very limited.

Sons of Union Veterans (1907)

Not to be confused with the Sons of Union Veterans of the Civil War, this Sons of Union Veterans was organized on October 7, 1907 in Cincinnati, Ohio. Their only known chapter was named the Fred H. Alms Commandery # 1. Comrade Alms for whom the chapter was named was a millionaire merchant and member of Fred C. Jones GAR Post # 401 of Cincinnati, Ohio. No records of their organization have been located so we do not know why they splintered from the Sons of Veterans of the United States of America. They did erect a memorial to Comrade Alms and participated in the Cincinnati Memorial Day observance until the early 1940s funded by the Alms estate.

Sons of War Veterans

Just as the Sons of Veterans of the United States of America were affiliated with the Grand Army of the Republic, so the Sons of War Veterans were the Sons' auxiliary of the Union Veterans Union. The Union Veterans Union had a membership of approximately 6,000 so their sons auxiliary must have been extremely small. Local units were referred to as a "Command".

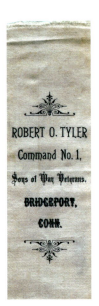

Only a membership ribbon has been found. It is possible due to their small size that no badges ever existed.

The Badges and Insignia of
the Grand Army of the Republic,
Sons of Union Veterans of the Civil War,
and the
Military Order of the Loyal Legion
of the United States

 83

Collector's Guide To The Membership and Officers Badges and Insignia Of The GAR, their Sons and the Loyal Legion.

In this book, we are attempting to assign a standard numbering sequence to all membership badges. **Type Ia** is the very first badge issued for an organization. **Type Ib** is a variation created by the manufacturer of the same issue or design. A variety is an item carrying a distinctive design. For an item to be considered a variety different from another variety, it must have a describable difference, such as in size, color, or design. Ribbons are not usually considered cause for a separate variety or type of badge. The same badge could have a membership ribbon, but changes to department or national ribbon while serving as an officer then revert to the membership ribbon upon leaving office. The exception is when a ribbon is a permanent usage change such as an Associate badge or a Junior Member badge in the Sons or the blue, red, or gold edged flag ribbon used by the GAR, Ladies of the GAR, or the Daughters. The ribbon alone is used to signify a different badge and once removed, its pin bar and pendant becomes parts of a previous variety.

A few terms will be constantly used:

Obverse - is the front of the badge pendant.

Reverse - is the back of the badge pendant.

Pin Bar - refers to the top bar, the clasp or top suspension. It refers to the bar at the top of the ribbon that has the pin on the back. Often it contains lettering or the name of the organization.

The pendant - is the medallion at the bottom of the badge.

The ribbon - usually connects the pin bar to the pendant, but chains or links may be used instead. Alternatively, the ribbon may simply back the badge. In a few cases, the author has chosen not to assign numbers and letters for varieties as they are one-of-a-kind handcrafted creation so each is therefore unique.

Membership Badges of the Grand Army of the Republic

As the GAR was organizing the need for a means to recognize members was acknowledged, but what this badge would ultimately look like was yet to be determined.

A prototype badge made from a United States Quarter may be the first concept for a GAR badge or perhaps just the artistic expression of an early member. Either way it is a rare example.

(Courtesy of Everitt Bowles)

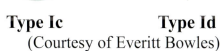

| Type Ia | Type Ib | Type Ic | Type Id |

(Courtesy of American Numismatic Society)   (Courtesy of Everitt Bowles)

Type Ia - In 1866, the 3 BN badge was adopted by the National Encampment to be the official insignia of the GAR. This badge was offered in a choice of silver plated for seventy-five cents; gold plated for $1.50; silver plated with a hinge pin for $1.75; or solid 18 kt. gold for $6.00 each.[92] The Grand Army Badge Manufacturing Company of Lafayette, Indiana, officially produced it and owned the copyright to the design.

Type Ib. Enameled varieties using a similar design were produced by B.T. Hayward of New York, NY.

Type Ic. Individually engraved varieties from local jewelers have also been found.

Type 1d. A hammered gold and enamel variation. Not hallmarked, but similar to those produced by B. T. Hayward of New York.

 85

On the reverse of the badge were screw posts, pin backs, or loops to sew it to the uniform. Roger Heiple, a noted GAR collector, owns one example adapted as a man's tie stickpin.

Few members of the Allied Orders or collectors have ever seen this badge. It must be considered one of the rarest of the GAR badges.

Robert Beath in his 1888 *History of the Grand Army of the Republic* states the symbolism on the badge is well known to those who were members in 1866 to 1869, but fails to explain it.[93] *The History of George Meade Post No. One, Dept. of Pennsylvania, GAR,* published in 1889 states: "The first badge adopted was a shield, upon which was engraved the insignia of the different arms of the army, the navy, and flags; also the letters 3BN-GAR, meaning "Third Battalion" Grand Army of the Republic."[94]

The badge was in the form of a modified shield 18mm x 15 mm in size or only five-eights of an inch to seven-eights of an inch high. The symbols include crossed American flags, an open Bible placed upon the flag with crossed swords upon the open Bible. The same motifs are outlined in the original GAR ritual for the altar. At the top of the badge are crossed rifles, a cannon, and an anchor representing the defense of the nation and the letters 3 BN, GAR.

Kenneth Johnson and Jeffery Floyd in their 1997 book, *Membership and National Encampment Badges of the Grand Army of the Republic*, gave the most plausible explanation of the letters:

"During the Civil War, a regiment consisted of two battalions. Once the enlistment of the regiment was over, whether three months or three years, the regiment could re-form with its original number, if sufficient veterans reenlisted. These veterans became a third battalion and were veteran volunteers. In battle, the third battalion stood behind the first two battalions to steady them. After the war, the GAR saw themselves as part of the shield of the Union. The regular army was the first battalion, the militia the second battalion, and the GAR as the third battalion or veteran volunteers."

Type II. It was adopted in 1868. This badge added an American bald eagle to the top of the shield shaped **Type I** badge. Officers' badges were authorized with insignia of rank attached to the bottom of the shield. Prices for this badge ranged from forty cents to $25.00. Due to production problems, the contracts were canceled and a new committee to select a new design was appointed.[96] Shown here is a prototype badge in partially completed state. No **Type II** badges were authorized for issuance to the general membership.

Type III. This was adopted by the GAR on October 27, 1869, and officially described on February 18, 1870.[97]

(Courtesy of Everitt Bowles)

Comrade Albert Leathers of Wakefield, Mass. wearing his type III badge.

"Description of the Badge:

The badge is of bronze, made from cannon captured in different decisive battles during the late rebellion, and in form a five-pointed star, similar in design to the two hundred Medals of Honor authorized by act of Congress to be given to soldiers and sailors most distinguished for meritorious and gallant conduct during the late war. The design, as here given, and adopted by the Grand Army of the Republic, was arranged by General F. A. Starring, Inspector General of the Order.

"**The Obverse.** In the center of the badge is the figure of the Goddess of Liberty, representing LOYALTY; on either side a soldier and a sailor clasping hands, representing FRATERNITY; and two children receiving benediction and assurance of protection from the comrades, representing CHARITY. On each side of the group are the National Flag and the Eagle, representing FREEDOM, and the Axe and Bundle of Rods, or Fasces, representing UNION.

"In each point of the star is the insignia of the various arms of the service, viz: the Bugle for Infantry, Crossed cannon for Artillery, Crossed muskets for the Marines, Crossed Swords for the Cavalry, and the Anchor for Sailors. Over the central group are the words 'Grand Army of the Republic', and under, the words and figures, '1861-Veteran-1866', commemorating the commencement and close of the rebellion and the date of organization of the Order.

"**The Reverse side** represents a Branch of Laurel - the crown and reward of the brave - in each point of the star. The National Shield in the center, surrounded by the twenty-four recognized Corps' Badges, numerically arranged, each on a keystone, and all linked together, showing they are united, and will guard and protect the Shield of the Nation. Around the center is a circle of stars, representing the States of the Union and the Departments composing the Grand Army of the Republic.

"**The Clasp** is composed of the figure of an Eagle, with Cross Cannon and Ammunition, representing Defense; the Eagle with drawn sword hovering over and always ready to protect from insult or dishonor the National Flag, which is also the Emblem and Ribbon of the Order."

The first of these badges were presented to the GAR national officers and numbered. This number appears on the bottom point of the star on the reverse side. General Frederick Starring who conceived the design received badge #1 according to his nephew. Very few badges were numbered in this manner.[98] This is not the serial number on the side of the star pendant. This side numbering that appears on **Type IV** and **Type V** badges was used to authenticate badges as coming from Grand Army Headquarters will be discussed shortly.

Please note the design of the **Type III** Grand Army of the Republic badge and compare it with the Civil War Congressional Medal of Honor. The similarities were intentional as the Grand Army saw all its members as heroic veterans. Mr. A. Demarest

Medal of Honor

of New York was the first jeweler designated to produce these badges and produced approximately 25,000 badges during the period 1869 to 1876. He was replaced as the official jeweler because it was discovered he was using bronze blanks rather than the captured Confederate cannon metal to produce the GAR medals as specified in his contract.[99]

The United States Mint at Philadelphia was the second official supplier of this style of GAR badges per GAR General Orders # 8 dated 24 December 1875. While the Mint produced the GAR badges, they used the actual Medal of Honor eagle die for the top of the GAR badges. At least one other manufacturer was producing badges under contract for the GAR during this period; D. B. Howell of New York, was paid for 2,500 badges. The GAR Headquarters paid thirty-two cents for each badge. This order was to be completed by May 30, 1877. Shortly after this a new contract was entered with Joseph Davison of Philadelphia. Davison would remain the official jeweler until 1946.

A one inch wide American flag ribbon was worn on all badges connecting the star pendant with the eagle pin bar.

The flag ribbon came in numerous varieties because replacement ribbons were obtained from nearly every badge manufacturer.[100] Noted manufacturers included Horstmann of Philadelphia, Pennsylvania (the official producer), M. C. Lilley Company of Columbus, Ohio, Annin Flag Company of New York, New York, and numerous badge manufacturers. It should also be noted that other organizations such as the United Spanish-War Veterans, the Patriotic Sons of America, the Junior Order of American Mechanics, and other fraternal lodges also used flag ribbon on their badges, and some Grand Army men might have used these ribbons on their GAR badges. So even greater variety can be found among original badges containing "original" ribbon. Correctly, the star pattern is located on left top of the ribbon. Many examples have been found with it on right top. These are simple manufacturing errors; if the bolt of flag ribbon was turned over as it was put on the machine the flag field comes off the bolt on the right instead of the left. There was no special meaning to the badge with a right sided star field other than a manufacturing error.

In 1873, the Department of Massachusetts proposed a change to the badge to identify present and past officers. Under this proposal, adopted by the National Encampment, solid color ribbons: buff (old gold) for national, cherry red for department, and medium blue for post would indicate the level of service while enameled miniature rank straps would indicate the position. The field of this rank strap for national and department officers was black, while the field on the post officers was bright blue enamel. The strap was approximately one-and-a-half inches long by one-half inch wide with a gilt edge one-sixteenth of an inch surrounding the enameled field. The miniature rank strap was placed at the top of the badge while the officer was serving in that position and moved to the middle of the badge upon leaving office to show past rank position.

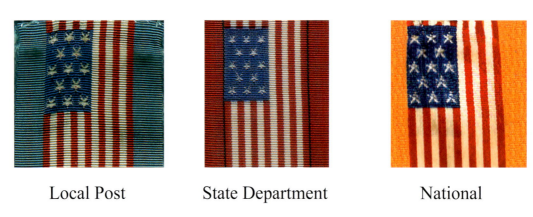

Local Post   State Department   National

Ribbons officially changed again at the 1886 National Encampment. The familiar American flag ribbon had a quarter inch colored border added to each side. The ribbon for officers was now one-and-a-fourth inches wide.[101] The border colors were blue (actually, copen blue) for posts. The Department ribbon was edged in cherry red (actually, a deep antique rose); for national officers the ribbon was edged in buff (actually, old gold) was used. For a brief transitional period the American flag ribbon was stitched to the solid color ribbon. Soon flag ribbon with the various border colors were woven and used for all officers. The GAR Officer's ribbon (blue, red, or gold edged flag ribbon) was patented in 1886 by Joseph Davison for the GAR, but only manufactured by Horstmann Brothers of Philadelphia, Pennsylvania, during the life of the GAR (1886-1940s). The cost of replacement ribbon when issued in 1887 was six cents.

For naval veterans, an anchor dangle was authorized to attach to the eagle clasp.[102]

Likewise, departments often attached a state symbol or corps badge as a dangle.

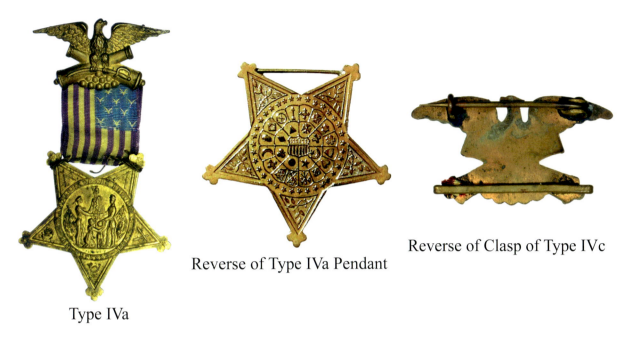

Reverse of Type IVa Pendant

Reverse of Clasp of Type IVc

Type IVa

Type IVa. On this badge the eagle clasp was altered so that both claws gripped the sword & cannon, the wings were lowered and straightened and the star pendant was made more symmetrical. The star pendant has laurel leaves in all five points on the reverse. Joseph Davison of Philadelphia manufactured these and all the official badges hereafter.

Type IVb. Likely a manufacturing error in 1876, some star pendants feature an incised star on each point rather than the normal raised star. Not illustrated.

Type IVc. The 1884 National Encampment approved a new design of the clasp with curved wings. The points of the eagle wings on **Type IVa** and **IVb** had a tendency to break thus the modification in design. The reverse of the clasp is blank.

Type V

Reverse of Type V Pendant

Reverse of Clasp of Type V

Type V. The 1886 National Encampment saw yet another set of changes to the badge. Additional corps emblems were added for Sheridan's, Wilson's, and Hancock's First Veteran Corps. These are located on the three lower points of the star on the reverse. [103]

On the reverse of the eagle clasp, a campfire with hanging cook pot was added and the patent dates of May 4, 1886, and June 22, 1886. This is the most commonly found badge as it continued in use until the last badges were issued in the 1940s. No records have been located as to when the last GAR badges were produced by Joseph Davison, but probably the late 1920s or early 1930s as posts were closing and returning overstock of badges to national headquarters.

ALL GAR Membership badges issued from 1869 through the 1940s are dated 1866 on the obverse, the founding date of the organization, not the date of manufacture. Encampment badges will have the year of the encampment on the obverse.

GAR Commander-in-Chief Robert Beath points out that a number of captured cannon were cut up and alloyed with copper and zinc to produce the badges. Confederate cannon metal varied greatly in metal content and was the source for numerous manufacturing problems causing damage to the dies. In 1884, Beath reported "90,500 membership badges had been issued during the (past) year. Through the kind courtesy and attention of Honorable Robert T. Lincoln, Secretary of War, and General Stephen V. Benet, more than ten thousand pounds of captured cannon-metal had been secured for the manufacture of badges."[104] Records indicate the supplies of captured cannon, however, were exhausted by the late 1880s and bronze blanks were used after that period. A pressure of 200 tons was required to stamp out the star pendants of the badge. [105]

The metal in the badges varied somewhat from manufacturer to manufacturer and cannon to cannon so variations in color should be expected. Manufacturers included A. Demarest of New York, D. B. Howell of New York, the U.S. Mint at Philadelphia and finally Joseph K. Davison & Sons of Philadelphia. Other manufacturers, as sub-contractors to Davison, may have been enlisted to meet demand at peak times. Joseph Davison and Sons was always the "official jeweler" from the 1880s until 1946 when Davison went out of business. August C. Frank and Company purchased Davison in 1946 and was named the next "official jeweler" to the Allied GAR Orders.

While various uniform companies offered the Grand Army buttons, flag replacement ribbon, hat wreaths, and a variety of uniform items, all badges were to be purchased from GAR headquarters only or the member might face expulsion from the Order.

On the side of the star pendant a letter and serial number is often seen, the letter stood for the first initial of the Commander-in-Chief's last name. Unfortunately, as letters duplicated (Warner in 1889 and Weissert in 1893) the system became limited for dating purposes. The numbers were repeated every year with the initial changing. Pendants for officer's badges were usually not numbered. Both numbered and

unnumbered badges are commonly found and both are authentic. **There were no records kept as to whom each numbered badge was presented.**

National and Department Inspectors, were trained and "inspected" badges to confirm they were authentic. Commander-in-Chief John Kountz at the 1885 National Encampment reported:

"The sale of badges provides a large revenue, which saves the necessity to increase the per capita tax, and thus every comrade is pecuniarily interested in procuring badges through National Headquarters.

John Kountz

Every comrade should feel a just pride in wearing a badge manufactured from captured cannon, and in no other way can they obtain a genuine captured-cannon badge." [106]

Commander-in-Chief Samuel S. Burdett in 1886 states, "The number of membership badges issued during the (past) year was 66,393. General Orders were issued as directed by the previous Encampment, to suppress the sale of spurious badges."[107] The 1886 Encampment went on to pass a resolution: "That the design of a badge recently patented…be, and the same is hereby, adopted as a membership badge of the Grand Army of the Republic; and that all comrades should in every case procure their badges from the proper Grand Army authorities."[108]

Samuel S. Burdett

Miniature Rank Straps with BLACK Background: [109]

Four Silver Stars - Commander-in-Chief

Three Silver Stars - Senior Vice Commander-in-Chief

Two Silver Stars - Junior Vice Commander-in-Chief

Two Silver Stars - Department Commander

One Silver Star - National Staff of Commander-in-Chief
  (Adjutant General, Quartermaster General, Surgeon
  General, Inspector General, Judge Advocate General)

One Silver Star - Senior Vice Department Commander

One Gold Star - Junior Vice Department Commander

Silver Eagle - Department Staff and Aide-de-Camp on
  the National Staff

Silver Leaf - Assistant Inspector General, Aide-de-Camp
  Department Commander Staff

Cross and a Single Star - National Chaplain

Cross only - Department Chaplain

Letter "C" - Council of Administration

Miniature Rank Straps with BLUE Background

Silver Eagle - Post Commander

Silver Leaf - Senior Vice Post Commander

Gold Leaf - Junior Vice Post Commander

Gold Leaf - Post Surgeon

Two Gold Bars - Post Officer of the Day

One Gold Bar - Post Adjutant or Post Quartermaster

Blank Field - Officer of the Guard

Cross - Post Chaplain

Letter "C" - Council of Administration

Sergeant-Major Chevron - Assistant Adjutant

Quartermaster Sergeant Chevron - Assistant Quartermaster

While the enameled chevrons are listed on the GAR Quartermaster Requisition form from national headquarters, they are not illustrated in the Blue Book or Constitution.

Their position, however, is listed in the Fourth edition of the Grand Army Bluebook dated January 1888 and they are illustrated in military supplier's catalogs of the period. Only very large posts would have had the position of assistant adjutant or assistant quartermaster and for that reason alone they are rare.

Miniature rank straps with red, yellow, light blue, and white backgrounds have been offered for sale as GAR. They are United Spanish-War Veterans miniature rank straps made after 1898 and were never used by the Grand Army of the Republic.

Presentation Past Officers Badges

Numerous military suppliers offered stock presentation badges for past Post Commanders and Past Department Commanders. These were available in sterling silver, gold filled, 10kt and 14kt gold. This illustration of a Past Department

Commander's badge is from an 1893 military supplier's catalog which lists the prices of: $111.50 in 14 kt, $93.00 in 10 kt. and $47.60 for sterling. The Past Post Commander's badge on right was made by Joseph Davison in 10 kt gold around 1900.

Additional varieties were custom made by the finest of jewelers in solid gold or gold and silver combinations often with the addition of rubies, sapphires and diamonds. The presentation and testimonial badges in the early years were truly a treasure. They became simpler in design and value as the membership declined.

GAR Lapel Button

A round bronze button was worn on the left lapel of civilian suits as a recognition button. It is copper bronze with the central design from the badge: a figure of Liberty, a soldier, a sailor, flags, armament, and children. The words, "Grand Army of the Republic 1861 Veterans 1866". Some have plain backs. After 1886, most have a cook pot over campfire on reverse of the same design that appears on the back of the membership badge pin bar. This is the only "official" lapel button.[110] The "cook pot" design may have been added to the lapel button to distinguish the official ones from the copies offered by military vendors. The original cost was only $1.00 a dozen or three dozen for $2.00 in 1896.[111] Silver and gold plated versions exist, but are not listed in official regulations and may have been presented as testimonials for Past Department Commanders or Past Commanders-in-Chief. Star shaped lapel buttons were ten cents each in bronze and fifteen cents each in gilt, but are not listed as "official" lapel buttons in any GAR regulations. The veterans held this button in high regard as noted in the following poem.

"The Little Brown Button" [112]

By John L. Parker (1837-1917)

The Little Brown Button,

The sacred bronze button;

The Grand Army Button

He wears on his coat.

"How much did it cost?"

Said a man to the soldier,

"That flat little button

Your wear on your coat?"

"Ten cents in good money."

He answered the stranger,

"And four years of marching

And fighting to boot."

The wealth of the world

Cannot purchase the emblem

Except that the buyer

Once wore the brave blue;

And it shows to mankind

The full marks of a hero:

A man, who to honor

And Country, was true.

Regulation Bronze
Button

Gold Plated
Testimonial Button

 97

The GAR Uniform

Each Post was allowed to specify a uniform for its members when on parade or formal ceremonial occasions. Usually this consisted of a federal blue single breasted coat with four or five GAR brass coat buttons down the front and two smaller buttons on each sleeve at the cuff. Officers might choose a double-breasted coat with more brass buttons. A blue slouch hat was worn with a hat wreath in either gold metal or embroidered versions. Dark blue trousers with a belt of either black leather or white webbing with a brass GAR belt buckle. Officers would have a GAR sword. The regulation membership badge was always worn on the left breast along with an assortment of other badges the wearer had earned.

Commander-in-Chief John Inman

Post and Department Badges

Wealthy posts and many Departments showed local pride by producing and wearing a local post badge or a department badge. Each was locally designed so each one is different. The relative wealth of the post or department determined design and material. Many wealthy organizations featured enamels and gold or silver plate. All bronze or brass badges may be selected by organizations struggling with a budget and many posts had no separate badge from the regulation membership badge.

Rhode Island Post 17   Massachusetts Post 5   New York Post 140   Kansas Department

GAR Funeral Badge - the real GAR Death Badge

For Memorial Day and funerals, a Post silk memorial ribbon would be worn. This ribbon was a somber black satin or silk with silver or gold lettering and fringe. The degree of complexity reflected the relative wealth of the Post. For other patriotic holidays or reunions, a more colorful silk ribbon identifying the Post might be worn. GAR headquarters issued badges, but numerous firms made silk ribbons. Each spring the Post would be flooded by new offers to sell them Memorial Day and memorial ribbons. Leading among these was Whitehead and Hoag Company of

Newark, New Jersey; Henderson-Ames Company of Kalamazoo, Michigan; Ehrman Manufacturing Company, Milford, New Hampshire; Torsch and Lee Company, Baltimore, Maryland; R. Carleton Company, Omaha, Nebraska; M. C. Lilley and Company, Columbus, Ohio; Baltimore Badge Supply, Baltimore, Maryland; Minks Badge Company, Baltimore, Maryland; and Walter Brunt of San Francisco, California. These are major suppliers and I am certain many more local and regional suppliers existed.

GAR Hat Wreath

The front of the slouch hat, or occasionally a kepi, featured a memorial wreath of thin stamped brass with letters in silver plate or plain brass reading "GAR". The metal version cost ten cents each or seventy-five cents a dozen while the gilt wire embroidered wreath was offered for fifty cents each in 1896.[113] Some would say the silver letters in a brass wreath was for officer's use, but official regulations do not indicate this. Most likely, it was a fancier version costing a few cents more for those who could afford it. Sometimes, a Post number or Department name was added above the letters "GAR".

GAR Belt Buckle – A sampling

The GAR belt buckle was usually cast brass three inches wide by two inches high. Popular designs included the GAR star with letters G.A.R., or variations of the three intertwined letters GAR in script or block letters. A number of variations do exist. Some officers wore the M 1851 US Army sword belt buckle: a three inch by two inch brass buckle with a large US eagle in the center surrounded by a brass or silver applied wreath.

M 1851 Reproduction

GAR Coat Buttons

All the major button manufacturers, Waterbury, Horstmann, Scovill, Lilley, and others with no markings at all manufactured GAR brass buttons. The button design was simply the letters GAR intertwined and came in a coat button one inch in diameter and in a half-inch vest or cuff button size.

GAR Jewelry and Souvenir Pins

As noted earlier, a national Grand Army encampment provided unlimited opportunities for unofficial and official souvenirs. Numerous stickpins, miniature badges, cuff links, and enameled pins bearing the GAR badge, small canteens, the GAR eagle from the badge clasp, or the GAR star were manufactured and sold to the visiting veterans. Local jewelers would offer gold and silver GAR keepsakes just as today's jewelers offer various lodge jewelry with Masonic or Knights of Columbus designs. Probably hundreds of different designs exist offering a delight to collectors.

Stick Pins   Miniature Badges   Cuff Links

GAR Silver Souvenir Spoons

Silver spoon collections were extremely popular among the Victorians. Almost every national encampment from the 1890s to the turn of this century had silver GAR spoons. The handle might feature a musket or the badge itself while the bowl of the spoon might feature important buildings from the encampment city or perhaps the local Civil War monument. As these were souvenirs, several patterns for the same year can be found. Issued price in the 1890s was fifty cents to one dollar for silver plated and $1.50 to $2.00 for sterling silver. In addition to the encampment, local events like the dedication of a Civil War monument or the death of a popular general might result in additional spoon designs.

1894   1895   1898   Monument   1976
Pittsburgh   Louisville   Cincinnati   Dedications   Columbus

GAR Paper Items

Ephemera is the term for printed-paper materials and with thousands of members, this field is unlimited. Membership certificates, memorial charts and prints bearing the GAR badge, printed General Orders, Department and National proceedings, political literature, forms, calling cards, and books of all sorts exist for the collector.

GAR and Sons Postcards

The turn of the century witnessed another Victorian custom of sending postcards for every holiday. Clapsaddle and Tuck were the two largest manufacturers. Each made more than a dozen GAR, Woman's Relief Corps, Ladies of the GAR and Sons of Veterans postcards. Some feature the brave soldiers in their youth; others reflect the advancing age of the soldiers with gray haired veterans honoring their fallen comrades. Postcards were made for Memorial Day, Lincoln's Birthday, and the Fourth of July. Condition determines value. Most collectors should seek mint crisp cards without bends or folds, missing corners, or ink stains. Nice examples can still be found in the $5 to $10 range. Ask to see postcards at antique shops and shows, but check all the possibilities. In addition to the above holidays, you should check: Americana, patriotic, military, soldiers, sailors, or GAR.

Stationery and Encampment Postal Covers

Letterhead and envelopes were necessary to conduct the business of the organization and numerous examples of the high degree of engraving can be found.

The final encampment of the GAR in 1949 saw the release of the GAR postage stamp (Scott's # 985). This resulted in numerous First Day of Issue covers.

Commemorative postal covers increased in popularity in the 1930s and although the GAR membership numbers were greatly diminished, stamp collectors began creating National Encampment envelopes. Several examples are illustrated here. This practice still occurs in the Allied Orders as witnessed by a 1970 SVR cover.

Visiting Cards

Today they are often mistakenly called business cards, but the Victorians had a quaint custom of presenting calling cards that bore their name only or possibly their name and organizational affiliation to announce their arrival or as a reminder of a meeting. Since both the Grand Army of the Republic and the Sons of Veterans did not endorse one member's business over another member, business cards did not normally feature GAR or SV emblems.

Cards for all the Allied GAR Orders and the Military Order of the Loyal Legion can be found and could be collected. Grand Army officer's cards feature embossed badges in full color with the highest past rank featured on the badge. Some photo cards exist with a picture of the veteran. While they originally cost one to two dollars per hundred, many visiting cards today sell between ten and fifty dollars. Of course, famous Civil War officers and past commanders-in-chief can bring premium prices.

National Encampment Badges

The first national encampment badges appeared in 1883 and were simply designed. By 1896 very elaborate three or four part metal badges ranging from six to eight inches in length were presented to the official Delegates or Representatives to the National Encampment by the host city. Since only 600 to 1500 men might be official delegates,[114] numerous souvenir badges were also made and sold. Each national encampment committee (parade, campfire, press, the Boy Scouts) might have its own separate badge or pin. Reunion meetings held at the national encampment and badges for the five Allied Orders add even more variety. A set of badges for just one national encampment could develop into a collection of a couple of dozen badges. One of the most sought after national badges is the 1949 GAR National Encampment, the last encampment of the GAR, as there were only six veterans attending. The badge is more common than suspected as 1500 were made and given to all the Allied GAR participants.

Every Department issued badges for its state encampment (convention) and many souvenir badges were made for various official and unofficial GAR events such as Memorial Day ceremonies, monument dedications, and reunions. This area of collecting alone could number into thousands of items and hundreds of printed pages.

Cincinnati, OH
1898

Rochester , NY
1911

Boston, MA
1917

Rochester , NY
1934

Indianapolis, IN
1949

Philadelphia, PA
1899

GAR Associates and Contributing Members:

GAR membership was open only to those who had an honorable discharge from the Federal government with service during the Civil War. National GAR regulations expressly forbid Posts from having associate memberships.

The 1884 National GAR Encampment adopted the following resolution,

"Membership is restricted to a single class, and to the exclusion of all others, such as Honorary, Associate, and Contributing members". [115]

There are several types of GAR associate memberships that have been discovered. The first was for financial reasons. Posts, especially in the larger cities, did have associate membership open to those who financially contributed to the support of the Post or their programs. The second reason was of a social nature and dealt with members who wanted to retain their ties with former comrades after they relocated to a new community. A member was required to transfer his membership from his "old" post to a "new" post if he moved. Some posts created associates to allow former members to retain their ties with their "old" post by becoming an Associate of their "old" post while transferring their full membership to a "new" post.

Special "associate" badges and lapel pins were always unique, as an associate could not wear the regulation GAR membership badge reserved for full members. Since all "associates" badges are non-regulation, each was made locally and a number of different designs exist.

Likewise, honorary membership was forbidden. The National GAR Encampment made one notable exception. They elected Clara Barton, founder of the American Red Cross, to honorary GAR membership due to her efforts in providing medical care during the war, her efforts to locate missing persons after the war, and the marking of veteran's graves at Andersonville, Georgia Union prison cemetery.

The Sons of Veterans and Sons of Union Veterans of the Civil War Membership Badges

Philadelphia Faction Sons of Veterans (Cadet Corps)

| Type Ia | Type Ib Obv | Type Ib Rev | Type II | Type III |

Type Ia. The badge used by the Philadelphia faction of the Sons consisted of a GAR star. Around the GAR central motif of the figure of Liberty, a soldier, a sailor and children are the words "Sons of Veterans 1861 to 65". The top pin bar is a one inch wide scroll with interlocking letters "SV". These were made in bronze. The ribbon is a red, white, and blue stripe. Most are found with no hallmark.

Type Ib. As above with the reverse hallmarked, "Pat. Ap'd. For # c 1043."

Type Ic. As above with a keystone hallmark on reverse and the words "Instituted SV April 24, 1879" on reverse. Not illustrated.

Type II. The same design as **Type Ia** re-struck using original dies for the 1956 National Encampment of the Sons of Union Veterans. This badge is a golden brass color. The ribbon is red, white, and blue stripe. There is no hallmark. Manufactured by August Frank, Philadelphia, Pa.

Type III. Pendant is the same design as **Type Ia**. Top pin bar is one and one fourth inch wide. It looks like antiqued copper. It was re-struck in 1995 for the benefit of the GAR Museum in Philadelphia, Pa. It has a hallmark consisting of a shield containing the letter "S". It is manufactured by Simons Brothers.

Type Ia Obverse

Type Ia. This badge consists of a circular pendant with a ten pointed star, a central motif of interlocking letters "SV" and the Latin words "Veteranorum Filii".

The top pin bar is semi-circular design consisting of a horizontal cannon with the date, 1880. Crossed rifles, crossed swords, and the rising sun appear behind the rifles. A drape contains their motto in Latin, "Gratia Dei Servatus" translated as "Preserved By the Grace of God". The pendant appears flattened. Originally badges were issued with the GAR flag ribbon. Badges found with a red, white, and blue stripe ribbon are a modern replacement for the original ribbon. There is no hallmark.

It is interesting that both the Sons in Pittsburgh and their rivals in Albany chose the same motto.

Type Ib. Possibly a change in manufacturer or process, the pendant appears more rounded before the design was struck into the brass blank. There is no hallmark. Not illustrated.

Type II. Circular pendant with 10 pointed star as in **Type Ia**. Three brass chain links connect pendant to the top pin bar. Date on cannon reads "1882". Back of top bar has a horizontal bar to hold ribbon directly beneath pin. This badge may have been used as a Department Encampment badge or used in the New Jersey Department. There is no hallmark.

Post System Lapel Button. A three-fourth inch bronze lapel button in the same design as the Post System badge pendant. There is no hallmark.

Type II Obverse
(Ronald Bellenger)

Post System Officer's Badges and Past Officer's Badges

Due to the size of the organization and its short life of eight years, officers' and past officers' badges are rare. The blue edged post ribbon, red edged department ribbon, or buff edged national ribbon was used with miniature rank bars to indicate an officer's position. Past officers wore the miniature rank strap at mid-point on their badge ribbon similar to the GAR use.

The examples illustrated are the Post Officer of the Day and the Past Senior Vice Commander-in-Chief's badge. The Officer of the Day is a Captain's rank on blue background rank strap with blue edged post ribbon. The Past Senior Vice Commander-in-Chief has a miniature rank strap with black background and three stars and used with the buff edged national ribbon.

Post Officer of the Day

Sr. Vice Comdr.-in-Chief

Gold Plated Badges

Similar in design to **Type I** except gold plated with blue and red enamel. Original use of this design is unknown, but probably it was the Past Department Commander's badge. Woman's Relief Corps Past Department President Ada Mohr of Brooklyn, New York presented this badge each year with $10.00 in gold to a member of the New York Sons who recruited the most new members. Where she found the original badge is unknown and the practice continued until her death in November 1937. Her gift badges are engraved on the reverse "Presented by Ada Mohr, (date)". There is no hallmark.

Mohr Recruiting Award

Filii Veteranorum Belt Buckles

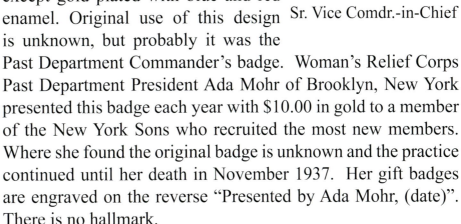

Sons' belt buckle consisted of interlocking letters "SV" in center with crossed arms and an anchor in the corners made of solid brass approximately two by three inches was likely used by the Post system headquartered in Albany, New York circa 1880s.

Another variety of belt buckle likely used by the Post system features a GAR Star design with the letters "SV" on either side of the GAR star. While no examples have been located, military supplier catalogs from the 1880s show this design. Circa 1880s. It is not illustrated.

SV and SOV Brass Buttons

Type I. Domed brass button with interlocking letters "SV" circle of stars around the edge. This design was used by the Post System of Sons from Albany, New York. Two sizes were issued: one inch coat buttons and one-half inch cuff or vest buttons. Circa 1880-1889.

Type II. Domed brass button with interlocking letters "SOV".

Transitional Badge

This badge was made with rose-gold and blue enamel. Its use is unknown, but probably a past camp officer's testimonial badge. There is no hallmark.

This example features a Maltese cross with two rifles crossed between the arms of the cross and behind a blue enamel SV monogram of the Post System in center. Name on pin bar reads "Col. Ellsworth Camp" and # 87 on lower arm of the cross. New York Sons Post # 87 was allowed to retain its name and number under the merger of 1889. So the term "Col. Ellsworth Camp" would indicate its issuance is after 1889 when it became a "camp" rather than a "post". The reverse is engraved with the name of honoree.

Sons of Veterans of the United States of America (Camp System)

"The Regulation badge shall be of bronze. On the face of the badge is a medallion with the monogram of the letters "SV" and the inscription "Gratia Dei Servatus MDCCCLXXXI" (Latin for Preserved By the Grace of God 1881, the founding date of the order, not the date of manufacture of the badge) the inscription being between two concentric circles of the medallion. The inner circle is enclosing the monogram and rays radiating from the center behind the monogram. Surrounding the medallion is a wreath of laurel and the ends of two cannons which apparently cross at the back of the wreath and medallion, and the top of the

 110

medal is surmounted by an eagle. The rectangular pin bar reads "Filii Veteranorum" (Latin for Sons of Veterans)."

| General Membership | Camp Officers | Division Officers | Grand Division Officers | National Officers |

Five ribbons for use on badges were prescribed and Major Augustus P. Davis copyrighted four of them in 1885. The four grosgrain ribbons were one and a quarter inches wide and consisted of a red, white, and blue edge with the broader center stripe. Deep blue center striped ribbon was used for elected Camp Officers, red center striped ribbon for Division Officers, white center striped ribbon for Grand Division Officers, old gold center striped ribbon for the Commandery-in-Chief Officers and the regulation membership badge was three vertical stripes of red, white, and blue.[117] These officers' ribbons were only to be worn while serving as an officer. Upon retiring from office, the member was supposed to return to the red, white, and blue striped membership badge ribbon.

Junior and ROTC   Associates   Junior Associates

Before 1900 the Grand Division ribbon was discontinued, but three additional ribbons are in use in 2014: a white grosgrain ribbon with two blue stripes on left and two red stripes on right. It is used on Junior Members badges and on ROTC badges. Solid royal blue ribbon is used for Associates and solid white ribbon for Junior Associates. While the Obverse is the same design, the Reverse of the badge differs from type to type.

Type Ia. On the REVERSE: a raised buckled belt with words "Filii Veteranorum". Inside the belt is a monogram of "USA". Fine print beneath reads: "patented June 27 '82 • B, B, & B" Manufactured by Bailey, Banks, and Biddle Jewelers of Philadelphia, Pennsylvania.

Numbered Type Ia Rev

Note: The first badges of **Type Ia** were numbered at the top just above the ring that attaches to the ribbon. No list has been found at Davis ★ Camp that records the badge number and recipient.

One example has been discovered that is numbered and gold plated. Perhaps it was the first membership recruiting incentive or a presentation badge from Maj. Davis.

Type I b. The design is the same as **Type Ia** "patented June 27 '82" along bottom of belt, but has no maker's initials. Official records indicate Bailey, Banks, and Biddle made this badge. Maj. Davis sold them to the Sons for thirty cents each.

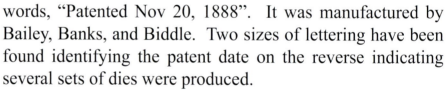

Type II Obverse

Type IIa.
The reverse consists of the full coat of arms of the Sons and the words, "Patented Nov 20, 1888". It was manufactured by Bailey, Banks, and Biddle. Two sizes of lettering have been found identifying the patent date on the reverse indicating several sets of dies were produced.

Type Ib Reverse

Type IIb. The reverse consists of the full coat of arms of the Sons and the words, "Patented Nov 20, 1888" as in **Type IIa,** but made of a coppery base with dark finish. The copper shows through finish. It was made by Bailey, Banks, and Biddle.

Type IIa Reverse

Type IIb Reverse

Type IIIa   Type IIIb   Type IVa   Type IVb

Recruiting Incentive Badges

Type IIIa. It is the same as **Type IIa** except with a plated pale gold finish on both pendant and pin bar. It was manufactured by Bailey, Banks, and Biddle. This gold badge was presented by Major A. P. Davis for recruiting nine new members during 1888.[118]

Type IIIb. It is the same as **Type IIa** except with a plated pale gold pendant with bronze bar. It was manufactured by Bailey, Banks, and Biddle. This badge was presented by Major A. P. Davis for recruiting seven new members in 1888.

Type IVa. It is the same as **Type IIa** except with a silver plated pendant and bar. This badge was manufactured by Bailey, Banks, and Biddle and was presented by Major A. P. Davis for recruiting five new members in 1888. The badge often appears black due to tarnish today. Look for hints of silver and try polish on the back.

Type IVb. It is the same as **Type IIa** except with a silver plate pendant and bronze bar. This badge was manufactured by Bailey, Banks, and Biddle and was presented by Major A. P. Davis for recruiting three new members in 1888. The badge often appears black due to tarnish today. Look for hints of silver and try polish on the back.

Type V

Type V. This has an enameled design consisting of a ribbon scroll pin bar reading, "Filii Veteranorum", an American eagle with spread wings on rocks, and a SV shield design featuring crossed swords and stars. Ribbon is gray-blue with gold stripe on each side. This design is unlike any other badge. It was presented by Major A. P. Davis for recruiting twenty-five new members in 1888. It is 14 kt. gold and enamel. Reverse not hallmarked except "pat. May 10, 1887". It was manufactured by Bailey, Banks, and Biddle. Probably each badge was handcrafted. These badges are extremely rare.

Major Augustus P. Davis held the patents and was the sole supplier of all badges until 1893. He was given the title "Special Ordnance Officer" and reports to the 1887 National Encampment:

"I have distributed directly to the Divisions and Camps a large number of badges and other kindred supplies, such as ribbon, crosses, etc...." [119]

The Commander- in- Chief Walter Payne reported badges were available at a cost of $6.00 a dozen. [120]

Type VIa. This design is similar to **Type I** except it has a flat buckled belt on the reverse. At the bottom of the belt, the hallmark reads: "Chas. M. Robbins & Co. Attleboro, Mass". The tips of the eagle's wings appear to go behind the cannons. This design was introduced in 1893, when the Commandery-in-Chief started to supply badges rather than Major A. P. Davis.

Type VIa

Type VIb. This design is the same as **Type IVa** except the hallmark reads, "Robbins Co" next to belt buckle at lower left.

Type VIb

Type VIc

Type VIc. This design is the same as **Type IVa** except the hallmark is a simple "R" at bottom center

In 1903, the red, white, and blue vertical striped ribbon used for general membership was discontinued and the blue center striped ribbon previously used for elected camp officers became the ribbon of the general membership badge.

Type VIIa. The design is the same as **Type IVa** except the badge appears flattened the hallmark reads: "Chas. M. Robbins Co • Attleboro, Mass." along bottom of belt on the reverse. The tips of the eagle's wings appear in front of the cannon barrels on the obverse. This design was issued around 1907.

Type VIIa

Type VIIb

Type VIIb. The design is the same as **Type IVa** except the badge appears flattened. The hallmark reads: "Robbins Co • Attleboro, Mass." along the bottom of belt on the reverse. The tips of the eagle's wings appear in front of the cannon barrels on the obverse.

Type VIIc. The design is the same as **Type IVa** except the badge appears flattened and the hallmark reads: "Chas. M. Robbins Co • Attleboro, Mass." along the top of belt on the reverse. The tips of the eagle's wings appear in front of the cannon barrels on the obverse.

Type VIIc

Type VIId. This design is the same as **Type IVa** except the badge appears flattened. The words, "Joseph Davison" is stamped horizontally just below attachment loop on the reverse clearly indicating a change of manufacturer for this badge. Not illustrated.

Type VIII. This badge has a thicker appearance and a shiny surface (spray lacquered) brownish bronze finish. The reverse is the same as **Type IVa** except hallmarked, "Robbins Co • Attleboro, Mass" along bottom of belt. This badge was issued around 1912.

Type IX. This badge has a matte brownish bronze finish. There is no maker's name, but this is the finish used by Joseph Davison of Philadelphia. This badge dates circa 1915.

Type VIII

Type X. This badge has a matte brownish bronze pendant. There is no top pin bar; the pin is hidden on the back. This badge has a special ribbon with seven-sixteenth of an inch navy blue on either side of the rainbow center. This badge was manufactured by Joseph Davison for Pennsylvania Sons of Veterans Reserve units inducted into federal service during World War I. The medal's box and envelope are marked, "Eternal Flame".

Type IX

Type X

There is a matching Type X ribbon bar for military uniform with hidden pin .

Type X Ribbon

  116

Sons of Union Veterans Regulation Membership Badge

Type XI. A transitional badge issued before a new official design was adopted. On the front of pendant there is a SV monogram, but the motto "Preserved By the Grace of God" is in English rather than in Latin. This badge was probably issued around 1919-1920. The design was proposed in 1918 but failed to be adopted by the National Encampment. The manufacturer is probably Charles Robbins Company. Not illustrated.

Type XII. A transitional badge circa 1926. The front of pendant has SUV monogram with the motto in Latin "Gratia Dei Servatus" like **Type IXa.** Reverse says "Sons of Union Veterans of the Civil War" inside two concentric circles. The pin bar still reads "Filii Veteranorum". The manufacturer is probably Charles Robbins Company.

Type XII
(Courtesy Gary Gibson)

Type XIII

Type XIII. With the name change approved by the 1925 National Encampment of the Commandery-in-Chief, the pin bar now reads "Sons of Union Veterans of the Civil War". The pendant is a matte bronze and on the face of the badge is a monogram of the letters "SUV" and the English inscription "Preserved By the Grace of God • MDCCCLXXXI" design similar to **Type I** obverse. The reverse has two concentric circles rather than a belt with words "Sons of Union Veterans of the Civil War" and "USA" within the circles. The manufacturer is unknown, but probably Joseph Davison of Philadelphia, Pennsylvania, because of the bronze finish on the pendant. It was issued after Department ratification of the new name in 1926.

Type XIV. The pin bar reads, "Sons of Union Veterans of the Civil War". On the face of the badge is a monogram of the letters "SUV" and the English inscription "Preserved by the Grace of God • MDCCCLXXXI". The pendant has a bronze finish over copper. The reverse has two concentric circles with words "Sons of Union Veterans of the Civil War" and "USA" within the circles. The badges were probably made by Joseph Davison of Philadelphia. Not hallmarked. Not illustrated.

Type XV

Type XV. This badge is the same as **Type XIV** except pendant and pin bar are a shiny copper finish. No hallmark.

Type XVI. This badge is the same as **Type XIV** except pendant and pin bar are a brown bronze. It is not hallmarked, but the finish is the one used by Joseph Davison. It is not illustrated.

Type **. Due to the metal shortage caused by World War II, a bakelite (plastic) badge was proposed. No examples have been found so it is listed for information only.

Type XVII. This badge has a brown bronze finish on both the pendant and the pin bar. The reverse has fine print along the bottom reading, "Aug. C. Frank Co. Phila., Pa." Not illustrated.

Type XVIII. This badge has a uniform reddish bronze finish. Like Joseph Davison before them, the finish was sprayed on then baked to achieve uniform color. These badges are always hallmarked, "Aug C Frank Co., Phila, Pa".

Type XVIII

August C. Frank was a jeweler in Philadelphia, Pennsylvania, and produced badges for all the Allied Orders from 1946 through 1972. August Frank hallmarked all his badges. In 1972, the firm closed and representatives of the Allied Orders recovered their dies and placed them with new jewelers, but the dies were not altered. All badges manufactured between 1973 to 1987 are incorrectly hallmarked "Aug. Frank", but made by Albert Bachmann Jewelers of Philadelphia. It is nearly impossible to determine Bachman's badges so no number is assigned.

Badges made between 1988 and 2013 are often double hallmarked. The pendant still may be hallmarked "Aug Frank", but the pin bar may have a shield with "S" the hallmark of Simons Brothers.

Type XIX. This is the badge issued by the Sons of Union Veterans from the late 1980s through 2013. The pendant and pin bar have an antiqued copper finish. It is somewhat shiny indicating a sprayed on finish. The reverse is the same as **Type XVIII**. The die still bears Aug Frank hallmark, but are manufactured by Simons Brothers. A small "S" in a shield appears on some pin bars and on the reverse of some pendants.

Type XX. Beginning in January 2014, all badges are being manufactured by Erffmeyer and Son Company of Milwaukee, Wisconsin. The pin bar has been altered to allow the ribbon to pass though it rather than be sewn and the back of the pendant is blank except for the "Esco Milwaukee" hallmark. Example shown has the Department officer's ribbon.

Type XIX

Type XX

SV Miniature Rank Straps and Chevrons

The Camps, Divisions, Grand Divisions, and Commandery-in-Chief used miniature rank straps with their badges as well as full size shoulder straps to indicate officer's positions within the Order. These were similar to the ones as used by the GAR: black field for National, Grand Division, and Division officers; a blue enameled field for Camp officers. After 1890 full size blue cloth chevrons were used by Camp non-commissioned officers and black cloth chevrons by Division non-commissioned officers.

"Under no circumstances shall any officer be allowed to assume or continue the duties of any position of honor and responsibility in the Order, unless he shall show his right to the office, by wearing the insignia of his actual rank. A failure to do this, after a reasonable time to equip himself, shall be deemed ample grounds to question his authority, or to respect and obey him as his office would properly demand."[121]

Regulations call for the miniature rank straps to be worn horizontally on each side of the jacket collar. Later regulations place the miniature rank strap just above the membership badge while in office.[122] The 1889 Constitutions, Rules, and Regulations state "as evidence of past rank a single miniature rank strap shall be worn diagonally upon the left breast above and to the left of the regulation badge, indicative of the highest past rank. This shall apply to all officers, whether Commandery-in-Chief, Division, or Camp officers".[123]

These photos show their respective ranks: Major A. P. Davis with bestowed the honor of Past Commander-in-Chief wearing a four star miniature rank strap diagonally; William Russell, serving as Commander-in-Chief in 1895 with a four star rank strap worn horizontally with his regulation badge; and F. D. Eddy wearing a single star rank strap diagonally as Past Junior Vice Michigan Division Commander.

Past Commander-in-Chief   Commander-in-Chief   Past Mich. Jr. Vice Comdr.
A. P. Davis   William Russell   F. D. Eddy

The Iron Cross / Past Camp Commander's Badge

A brother who served the full term as Camp Commander or completed a term as Camp Commander was entitled to wear an Iron Cross. This cross shaped badge is symmetrical in shape one and one-fourth inch by one and one-fourth inch. The design of the badge pendant affixed to the center of the cross.

The 1887 Regulations state the Iron Cross, awarded after August 31, 1886, is for the Past Camp Commanders only and issued with Camp officer's ribbon.

Type I. The Iron Cross was painted with a satin black enamel paint when issued. There was no visible pin bar, but a hidden brass clasp affixed to the back of the ribbon at the top.

Type I

This **Type I** clasp reads "Maj. A. P. Davis, Pittsburgh, Pa", then features a row of stars with a large eagle with open wings holding leaves in its talons. These first Iron Cross badges were made by Bailey, Banks, and Biddle of Philadelphia, Pennsylvania and cost thirty cents each.

Type II. This Iron Cross badge was painted with a satin black enamel paint when issued. There was no visible pin bar, but a hidden

brass clasp affixed to the back of the ribbon at the top. The brass clasp simply read "Maj. A. P. Davis, Pittsburgh, Pa". These were made by Bailey, Banks, and Biddle of Philadelphia, Pennsylvania.

Type III. This Iron Cross badge has an oxidized silver color finish. The miniature badge pendant has the "SV" monogram. There was no visible pin bar and the simple brass clasp affixed on the back has no wording. This badge was manufactured by Charles Robbins Co. Attleboro, Massachusetts, beginning in 1893. There is no manufacturer's hallmark.

Type IV. This Iron Cross badge has an oxidized silver finish. The miniature badge pendant has the "SUV" monogram. There is no visible pin bar and the hidden clasp is plain brass. The bottom of the cross is hallmarked "Robbins Co., Attleboro, Mass" at the bottom.

Type III

Type IV

Type IV Reverse
with Robbins Hallmark

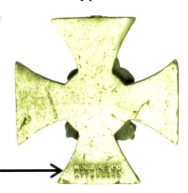

Type V. This Iron Cross badge has an oxidized silver finish. The miniature badge pendant has the "SUV" monogram. There is no visible pin bar and the hidden clasp is plain brass. There is no hallmark, but it was made by Joseph Davison of Philadelphia. Not illustrated.

Type VI. This Iron Cross badge has an oxidized silver finish. The miniature badge pendant has the "SUV" monogram. There is no visible pin bar and the hidden clasp is plain brass. These badges are hallmarked "Aug Frank, Phila" on the reverse at the bottom. They would have been manufactured between 1946 and 1972.

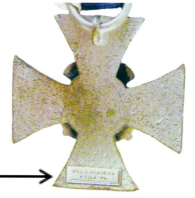

These Iron Cross badges are still hallmarked "Aug C Frank, Phila.", but were manufactured by Albert Bachmann of Philadelphia from 1973 to 1987. As the two appear the same, no number is assigned. ⟶

Type VI

Type VII. This Iron Cross badge has an antiqued shiny silver finish. The miniature badge pendant has the "SUV" monogram. There is no visible pin bar and the hidden clasp is plain brass. It was made by Simons Brothers.

This badge is hallmarked by Simons Brothers (S in shield)

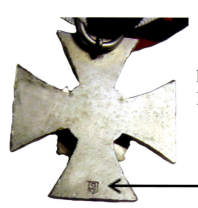

Type VII

Type VIII. Beginning in January 2014, all badges are being manufactured by Erffmeyer & Son Company of Milwaukee, Wisconsin. The hidden pin bar appears to be crimped in place rather than sewn. The "ESCO Milwaukee" hallmark is located at bottom of the cross on the reverse side.

Prior to August 31, 1886, the Iron Crosses were issued with Division ribbon (red), Grand Division ribbon (white) and Commandery-in-Chief ribbon (gold) to show past ranks of Past Division Commander, Past Grand Division Commander, or Past Commander-in-Chief. The Silver Cross for Past Division Commanders was adopted in 1886. The Gold Cross that was used for Grand Division Commander / Past Grand Division Commander's badge became the Meritorious Service and the Gold Star that had been used for Meritorious Service became the Past Commander-in-Chief's badge.

Past Division
Commander

Past Grand Division
Commander
(Courtesy Gary Gibson)

Past Camp Commander's Badge – in 14 Kt. Gold

There are a few notable exceptions when the "Iron Cross" was made in gold. These were always commissioned from a local jeweler and not issued by the national organization.

Type I   Type II   Type III   Type II with red enamel in center.

Type I. This cross shaped badge is symmetrical in shape one and one-fourth inch by one and one-fourth inch in 14 kt gold. The design of the Son's badge pendant affixed to the center of the cross is also 14 kt gold. The circular motif in the center of the pendant is blue enamel. The ribbon is the red Division ribbon. The pin bar is also made of 14 kt gold. In the center is a red enameled keystone and the words "Past Comdr". This badge was issued by Anna M. Ross Camp # 1 of Philadelphia.

Type II. This cross shaped badge is symmetrical in shape one and one-fourth inch by one and one-fourth inch in white enamel with 14 kt gold edge. The design of the Son's badge pendant affixed to the center of the cross is also 14 kt gold. The circular motif in the center of the pendant is blue enamel. In the center of the pin bar is a red keystone with the number "2" and the words "Camp S of V" in blue. The reverse was blank for engraving. This example dated 1908.

Type III. This cross shaped badge is symmetrical in shape one and one-fourth inch by one and one-fourth inch in 14 kt gold. The design of the Son's badge pendant affixed to the center of the cross is also 14 kt gold without enameling. The pin bar is also made of 14 kt gold. The ribbon is the blue centered membership ribbon. This particular badge was created by Tippin Camp 41 of Pottstown, Pennsylvania.

The Bronze Cross / Sons of Veterans War Service Badge

With the successful completion of the Spanish-American War, the Sons of Veterans authorized the issuance of a war service badge. Congress donated captured Spanish cannons to provide the bronze metal for the badge pendant.

Type I. This is a one and one-fourth inch by one and one-fourth inch Bronze Cross. Superimposed upon the bronze cross is a silver memorial wreath with a federal blue enameled center reading "Filii Veteranorum• MDCCCLXXXI" around a central monogram "USA" in the center. The badge has a slight dome shape and appears a heavier weight than later war badges. Red Division ribbon is used with no visible pin bar. There is no hallmark, but Charles Robbins was the official Sons jeweler at this time.

The reverse of the Sons of Veterans war service badge bears the words "Sons of Veterans USA War Service" and badges are individually numbered. This badge was authorized

Type I Obverse   Type I Reverse

for combat service by members of the Sons of Veterans who participated in the Spanish-American War.[124] A numbered certificate and numbered badge were recorded at the Sons national headquarters. These reference books were apparently lost when the Sons headquarters moved from Reading, Pennsylvania, in 1949.

Type II. This is a one and one-fourth inch by one and one-fourth inch Bronze Cross. Superimposed upon the bronze cross is a silver memorial wreath with a dark navy blue enameled center reading "Filii Veteranorum• MDCCCLXXXI" around a central monogram "USA" in the center. A red Division ribbon is used with no visible pin bar. The reverse has an individual number at the top, following with the words "Sons of Veterans U.S.A. War Service", then this hallmark "C M Robbins Co Makers Attleboro, Mass USA". This badge was authorized for World War I veterans. In 1926, the Commandery-in-Chief eliminated it saying, "It was discontinued upon supply depletion".

Type II Reverse

Type III. This War Service Badge was issued by the Sons of Union Veterans of the Civil War. In 1939, this badge was re-instituted and remains in use today. The design was slightly altered from the previous design. The Bronze Cross remained with a bronze memorial wreath, but the navy blue enameled center now reads "Preserved By the Grace of God and MDCCCLXXXI" and has "SUV"

in the center. Bars designating the period of service were established for World War II. It was manufactured by Charles Robbins, Attleboro, Massachusetts, or Joseph Davison of Philadelphia, Pennsylvania. The badges are no longer numbered.

Type III Obverse   Type III Reverse

Type IV. The Bronze Cross for war service was issued from 1946-1972 as well, and the Korean and Vietnam service bars were manufactured by August C. Frank Jewelers of Philadelphia, Pennsylvania. The design remains the same as **Type III** with a bronze memorial wreath. All badges bear the "Aug C. Frank, Phila, Pa" hallmark.

August C. Frank Hallmark ⟶

Type IV Reverse   Type IV Obverse

The Bronze Cross for war service badges issued between 1973-1987 were manufactured by Albert Bachmann Jeweler of Philadelphia, Pennsylvania, but still bear the Aug. C. Frank hallmark. As they cannot be determined from Aug. Frank, no number is assigned.

Type V. The Bronze Cross was altered again after 1988. The obverse design in bronze is the same as **Type IV**. The memorial wreath is silver again. On the reverse is a design made of two concentric circles with the words "Sons of Union Veterans of the Civil War", between the circles. "USA" is in the center with "War" at top of circle and "Service" at the bottom of circle. Manufactured by Simons Brothers.

Type V Obverse   Type V Reverse

A bronze bar may be purchased separately and attached to the Department ribbon designating the period of combat. There are no hallmarks on service bars.

Bronze Service Bars

Type VI. Beginning in January 2014, all badges are being manufactured by Erffmeyer and Son Company of Milwaukee, Wisconsin. They are hallmarked on the reverse "ESCO Milwaukee".

SV War Service Badge - Private Issues -

The example shown is a one inch round pendant badge. The obverse features a seated figure of Liberty with a small standing U.S. eagle. The words around the edge read, "United States Forces 1917-1918. The reverse reads, "Presented to _____ by the George A Custer Camp 11, Sons of Veterans, Whitman, Mass. in grateful recognition of patriotic service rendered in the World War." It has the Sons' blue camp ribbon. There is no visible pin bar. It is hallmarked "W & H Co" (Whitehead and Hoag Company of Newark, New Jersey).

127

Special note: During World War I, the Pennsylvania Sons of Veterans Reserve units inducted into federal service were presented with a special Sons of Veterans badge. **Type X**. With a matte brownish bronze pendant and no visible pin bar. There is a special ribbon with a seven-sixteenth inch navy blue color on either side of the rainbow center. It was made by Joseph Davison for Pennsylvania SVR units federalized into service during WWI. There is a matching ribbon bar for military uniform with hidden pin bar. The box and envelope are marked "Eternal Flame". Davison also produced the 28th Division, Pennsylvania National Guard Medal. The SVR units were part of the 28th Division.

28th Div.
Penn. National Guard

SV Type X

SUVCW Military Service Badge

In 2000, the National Encampment of the Sons revised their regulations with regard to the Bronze Cross / War Service Badge restoring its restriction to veterans in service during periods of combat only and the SUV regulations were amended to allow the creation of a military service badge.

The obverse is a one and one-fourth inches in diameter antiqued silver round pendant featuring two concentric rings with the words "Sons of Union Veterans of the Civil War" between them and a central motif consisting of a side view of an American eagle in flight holding a federal shield. The reverse reads "For Honorable Military Service".

Manufactured by Erffmeyer and Son Company of Milwaukee, Wisconsin. They are not hallmarked

The Silver Cross - Past Division / Past Department Commander's Badge

Type I. The Sons of Veterans Silver Cross consists of a *transparent red and opaque white enameled cross* on silver with four silver eagles facing left between the enameled cross. A small silver wreath frames an opaque blue enameled center. The words "Filii Veteranorum • MDCCCLXXXI" surround the letters "USA" in the center. A red Division ribbon is used with no visible pin bar. No hallmark, but manufactured by Bailey, Banks, & Biddle of Philadelphia, and cost $4.00 each. The reverse is simply marked "sterling". Some **Type I** badges were issued with a pin bar featuring the name of the recipient and the Division Corps badge attached as a dangle.

Type I

Type II. Beginning in 1893, the Silver Cross Badge was made by Charles Robbins of Attleboro, Massachusetts. The obverse design remained the same as type I. The reverse is hallmarked "Robbins Co., Attleboro Sterling".

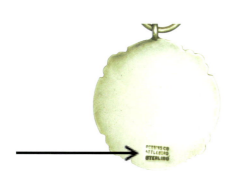

Type II

Type III

Type III. A variation of the Silver Cross that lacks the solid blue enamel in the center of the wreath illustrated in the regulations from 1905 through 1920, though some **Type II** badges have been found dated as late as 1913. These were probably made by Joseph Davison of Philadelphia.

Type IV. With the change of name to "Sons of Union Veterans of the Civil War" and the elimination of the Gold Cross, the Silver Cross was re-designed. The SUVCW Silver Cross consists of an *opaque red and white enameled cross* with four silver eagles facing left between the crossbars. A silver wreath with a ruby at top surrounds an opaque blue enameled center, the words "Sons of Union Veterans of the Civil War • MDCCCLXXXI" with "SUV" in center. The Department ribbon is used with no visible pin bar. This badge was made by Charles Robbins Company.

Type V. Beginning in 1946, the Silver Cross with the same design was made by August Frank Company of Philadelphia. The reverse was then hallmarked "Aug Frank Co., Phila." and "sterling".

Type IV & V Obverse

According to Sons' National Secretary, Chester S. Shriver,[125] in the late 1970s and early 1980's badges were silver plated rather than sterling due to the extremely high price of silver. Incorrectly, the reverse is still hallmarked "sterling". They were manufactured by Albert Bachman of Philadelphia. As they are still hallmarked Aug. Frank no number is assigned.

Aug. Frank hallmark

Type V Reverse

Type VI. The obverse is the same design as **Type III.** The reverse is hallmarked Simons Brothers. This hallmark is a shield containing an "S".

Type   VI

Type VII. In 2014 this badge will be manufactured and hallmarked by ESCO of Milwaukee, Wisconsin. Not illustrated.

Type VI Obverse

Silver Cross Presentation Badges

Although the official badges per national regulations have been described already, some Divisions and even the Commandery-in-Chief, had custom presentation badges made and presented to a beloved commander as a sign of love and respect. The addition of diamonds, sapphires, and rubies to embellish the badge was condemned by the Sons National Encampment in 1914, "That Divisions be instructed that the Past Division Commanders' badge presented by them must not be adorned with precious stones and further, that in the future, the badge presented to the Past Commander-in-Chief shall be strictly in accordance with that prescribed by the Constitution and Regulations".[126] All presentation badges were unique and handcrafted by a local jeweler. Here are several examples:

This 14kt gold Past Division Commander's badge, based upon the design of the Silver Cross, has the addition of six diamonds, one on each eagle's breast and two on the wreath, plus one ruby and one sapphire. This example came from the Division of Rhode Island and is engraved on the reverse "Presented to Commander Orray T. Mason, by the members, RI Division, Sons of Veterans, USA, July 2, 1904". Similar ones have been found for other Rhode Island Past Division Commanders. It is not hallmarked, but was manufactured by E. L. Louee and Company, Providence, Rhode Island.

This Past Division Commanders badge features gold eagles and a gold wreath; it was awarded by Major & Mrs. A. P. Davis to Commander-in-Chief George Abbott of Illinois December 25, 1887. Brother Abbott joined the Order in August 1884. He held several appointed positions until 1887, when he was elected Illinois

Division Commander. That August he was elected Commander-in-Chief and then again reelected the following year. He successfully led the effort to merge the "Post System" members into the Camp System in 1889. The gold pin bar reads: "G.B. Abbott" and has the Illinois Division corps badge attached as a dangle. This badge was made by Bailey, Banks, and Biddle Jewelers of Philadelphia.

Charles Messer
N Y Commander 1948
Commander-in-Chief 1961

The Department of New York retained this custom of having a personalized pin bar with the New York corps badge attached for all their Past Department Commanders. This example was presented to Charles Messer who served as New York Department Commander in 1948 and Commander-in-Chief in 1961.

Clearly in the 1880s, this procedure of adding a name bar and Division corps badge was the accepted standard. Today, the New York Department is the only Department still adding the corps badge to their Past Department Commander's badges. These were ordered through National headquarters so were made by the official jeweler at the time. The jeweler would have been one of the following: Bailey, Banks, and Biddle, Robbins, Davison, Frank, Bachmann, Simon Brothers, or ESCO.

Among the inventory sold by Mrs. A. P. Davis to the Sons Headquarters in 1899, following Maj. Davis's death, was a Silver Cross badge featuring a gold wreath. This may have been simply a prototype badge never put into production or may have been an unknown presentation badge which I have not located.

The Gold Cross - Past Grand Division Commander's Badge / Meritorious Service Award

Type Ia Obverse   Type Ib Obverse   Type II Illustration from 1905 regulations

Major A. P. Davis appointed influential GAR members as regional commanders of the Sons of Veterans, USA.[127] This position was short lived and only existed for 3 years. Divisions were then required to report directly to national headquarters.

Type Ia. The Gold Cross consisted of a *transparent red and opaque white* enameled cross with four gold eagles facing right between the enameled cross. These eagles have a base behind them. A small gold wreath frames an opaque red enameled center. The words "Filii Veteranorum• MDCCCLXXXI" on a white enameled ring surround the letters "USA" in gold on a red enameled center. The reverse is silver. There is no visible pin bar. The Grand Division ribbon was a white ribbon with red, white, and blue edging. Made by Bailey, Banks, and Biddle Jeweler of Philadelphia. Not hallmarked.

Headquarters' correspondence from Past Commander-in-Chief George Marks of the Post system states that his Gold Cross was copied from that of the Past Grand Division Commander Raphael Tobias, but "different" from the official pattern at Headquarters indicating very early variations.

Type 1b. Design as above except the gold eagles are cut out with no base behind them.

Type II. The Gold Cross illustrated in the 1905 regulations is the same as **Type Ib** except the free standing eagles are larger and facing left.

Type III Obverse

Type III. After the position of Grand Division Commander was eliminated in 1886, the badge continued to be awarded by the Commandery-in-Chief for Meritorious Service [128] from 1886 through 1912. These badges had the Commandery-in-Chief gold centered ribbon. The first ones were made by Bailey, Banks, and Biddle. The last ones were probably made by Robbins Co. None are hallmarked.

Original cost from Major Davis to the Sons was $11.00.

The Gold Star - Past Commander-in-Chief Badge

The original use of the Gold Star was for meritorious service. The Past Commander–in–Chiefs wore an Iron Cross with a Commandery-in-Chief gold ribbon. In 1887, national regulations restricted the Iron Cross to Past Camp Commander use and the Gold Star became the Past Commander-in-Chief's emblem.

The design of the Past Commander-in-Chief Gold Star shall be an eight pointed star with rays appearing to radiate from the center with a gold memorial wreath surrounding a silver eagle on a red enameled center. This Gold Star could be worn as a badge or from a neck ribbon worn just below the Adam's apple. Early versions are shown with four star rank strap attached at the top; upon leaving office the rank strap is worn diagonally above the regulation badge of the Order. Today, there is no visible pin bar.

Type I Illustration from 1905 regulations

 134

(Courtesy of
Gordon R. Bury)

Type I. Past Commander-in-Chief badges issued by the Sons of Veterans will have the words "Gratia Dei Servatus• MDCCCLXXXI"

Type II. Past Commander-in-Chief badges issued after 1926 by the Sons of Union Veterans of the Civil War will be same design except it will have words "Preserved by the Grace of God • MDCCCLXXXI"

According to National Secretary Chester Shriver, there were no dies for this badge. Each is handcrafted for the present Commander-in-Chief. Bailey, Banks, and Biddle, Charles Robbins, Joseph Davison, August Frank, G. A. and C. R. Schlechter, I. Bedichimer Co. and Simons Brothers are among the jewelers who handcrafted this badge. A die was created in 2014 for this badge.

Past Commander-in-Chief Presentation Badge

Commander-in-Chief
Maccabe

This is an example of a Past Commander-in-Chief presentation badge which was presented to Joseph Maccabe in 1893. It features six small diamonds and eight larger rubies. The badge is, of course, solid gold.

(Courtesy of
Ronald Bellenger)

SUVCW Fifty Years Membership Badge

A design contest was held in 1936 to create a Fifty Year membership badge. Charles Robbins of Attleboro, Massachusetts won the contest. The design consisted of a **Type XIV** membership badge pendant with a blank pin bar to be engraved with the member's name and a second bar reading, "Fifty Year Membership". The national ribbon with old gold center was used. The original cost in 1936 was $1.50.

Type I Obverse

Type I. The badge is as described above. It was manufactured by Charles Robbins, but there is no hallmark.

Type I Reverse

Type II Reverse

Type II. The badge is as described above. It was manufactured by August C. Frank and has the "Aug Frank, Phila." hallmark. These date between 1946 to 1972. Between 1973 to 1987 the badge was manufactured by Albert Bachmann, but with the "Aug. Frank, Phila." hallmark. There is no separate number assigned as they cannot be distinguished from the Aug. Frank issues.

Type III. The badge has the **Type XIX** membership pendant. It is manufactured by Simons Brothers and bears their hallmark of a shield containing an "S" on the top pin bar and fifty year membership bar. The pendant is still hallmarked "Aug C Frank, Phila." Overall the badge is a light copper color.

Type III Obverse

Type IV. Beginning in January 2014, all badges are being manufactured by Erffmeyer and Son Company of Milwaukee, Wisconsin. They are hallmarked on the reverse "ESCO Milwaukee". Not illustrated.

SUVCW Seventy and Seventy-Five Year Badges

In 1994, the National Organization authorized seventy and seventy-five year membership badges. They are the same design as the fifty year badge except the secondary bar reads "70 or 75 year Membership". These were never manufactured even though they are authorized.

Junior Order, Sons of Veterans, USA

A free form diamond shaped pin approximately one-half inch wide by three-fourths of an inch high. It has red enamel at top, a white band across the center, and blue enamel at the bottom. It is lettered in gold, with the words "Junior" on the red, "Order" on the white band, and "SV" on the blue. This may be the only membership device issued.

(Courtesy of
Gary Gibson)

SUVCW Junior Member

In 1994, a junior membership was established for boys between the ages of 8 to 13. At age 14, they become full members with full rights of membership. In 2001, the age for Juniors was lowered to 6.

Type I. The Sons Type XIX regulation bronze pin bar and pendant are used with a special ribbon consisting of two narrow blue stripes on the left of the white ribbon and two narrow red stripes on the right, to create this Junior Member's badge. It is manufactured by Simons Brothers.

Type II. Beginning in January 2014, all badges are being manufactured by Erffmeyer and Son Company of Milwaukee, Wisconsin. They are hallmarked on the reverse "ESCO Milwaukee." Not illustrated.

SV Associate Members Badge

Prior to 1954, there was no Associates class of membership, but like the GAR, local camps especially in the larger cities, elected "Associates" to those men who financially supported their programs. The Oliver Tilden Camp 26, Brooklyn, NY Associates badge is shown as an example of this practice. The badge is gold plated. The pin bar reads "Associate Member". A red, white, and blue vertical stripe ribbon was used. This example has a round scalloped pendant with the "SV" monogram, memorial wreath and words "Oliver Tilden Camp No.26•NY". No hallmark.

SUVCW Associate Badge

Associates were officially approved in 1953. This class of membership was open to men who had an interest in the organization, but lacked blood kinship to the Union Veterans. Originally, Associates had no voice in the affairs of the Order or voting rights. Today, the restrictions on Associates prevent them from

Type I Obverse   Type II Obverse

holding the office of Commander-in-Chief and Junior or Senior Vice Commander-in-Chief. There are also restrictions on the number of Associates who may be voted into membership.

Type I. The Associate badge consists of a **Type XVII** membership badge with "Associate" printed in silver diagonally across the front of a solid blue ribbon. They were manufactured by August Frank of Philadelphia and bear his "Aug Frank" hallmark on the reverse of the pendant.

Type II. Beginning in 1974, a plain dark blue ribbon was adopted for Associates badges. The pendant still has the "Aug C Frank" hallmark, but they were manufactured by Albert Bachmann from 1974 to 1987. There is no imprint on the ribbon.

Type III. The badge is a **Type XIX** pendant and bar with a solid bright blue ribbon. It is manufactured by Simons Brothers. There is no imprint on the ribbon. Most pin bars have an "S" within a shield hallmark.

Type IV. Beginning in January 2014, all badges are being manufactured by Erffmeyer and Son Company of Milwaukee, Wisconsin. They are hallmarked on the reverse "ESCO Milwaukee."

Junior Associates Badge

Type III Obverse

Type I. This badge was authorized in 2010 for Junior Associates. It consists of a **Type XIX** pendant and Bar with a solid white ribbon. It is manufactured by Simons Brothers. Most pin bars have an "S" within a shield hallmark.

Type I Obverse

Type II. Beginning in January 2014, all badges are being manufactured by Erffmeyer and Son Company of Milwaukee, Wisconsin. They are hallmarked on the reverse "ESCO Milwaukee".

SUVCW Honorary Member Badge

Type I. The Commander-in-Chief may confer "Honorary Membership" with approval of the Council of Administration upon those men & women "of acknowledged eminence who are especially distinguished for conspicuous and consistent loyalty" and are not known to be eligible for membership in our Order. At first, no badge was authorized for Honorary Members. In 1993, the National Encampment created an Honorary Member Badge. It consists of the pin bar and pendant of **Type XIX** with a solid blue ribbon and a half inch silver star attachment to the center of the ribbon. Most pin bars have an "S" within a shield hallmark as it is manufactured by Simons Brothers.

Type I Obverse

Type II. Beginning in January 2014, all badges are being manufactured by Erffmeyer and Son Company of Milwaukee, Wisconsin. They are hallmarked on the reverse "ESCO Milwaukee." Not illustrated

Major A. P. Davis Badge:

The badge consists of an oval pendant bearing the likeness of A. P. Davis, founder of the Sons of Veterans USA. The reverse reads: "Major A. P. Davis born Gardiner, Maine May 10, 1835." The pin bar is an elongated U.S. eagle with spread wings. The pin bar and pendant are made of antiqued bronze. Three different ribbons have been discovered (**Type I, II, III**). The badge bears the birth-date, but not the death date of the Sons' founder, Major A. P. Davis. Photos confirm that these badges were in use in the early 1890s, so the most probable usage was another recruiting award presented by Major Davis. Blue, red, and gold ribbons likely indicate increasing levels of members recruited. **Type IV** was awarded to participants at Major A. P. Davis's funeral. Probably all were produced by Bailey, Banks, and Biddle Jewelers of Philadelphia, Pennsylvania, as this was the jeweler Davis chose to manufacture all badges prior to 1893. They have no hallmark and each is listed as a separate variety because of the different ribbons used.

Type I Obverse   Type II Obverse   Type III Obverse
(Courtesy George Kane)

Reverse for
Types I through IV

Type IV Obverse

Type V Obverse

Type I. The eagle pin bar and pendant are as described on previous page with a blue/gray grosgrain ribbon edged in red and gold.

Type IIa. The eagle pin bar and pendant are as previously described with a red grosgrain ribbon with thin gold and blue edging.

Type IIb. The eagle pin bar and pendant are as already described with a red grosgrain ribbon, a single thin gold stripe on each side, and three thin gold stripes in the center of the ribbon. This badge is not illustrated.

Type III. The eagle pin bar and pendant are as described previously. It has a gold ribbon with red and blue edging.

Type IV. The eagle pin bar and pendant are as already described with a black grosgrain ribbon. In 1899, Mrs. A. P. Davis issued these badges to the members of the Sons that participated in her husband's funeral in Pittsburgh. An example with the black grosgrain ribbon is displayed at the Soldiers and Sailors Building in Pittsburgh, Pennsylvania. Not hallmarked.

Type V. On May 21, 1999, the centennial of Major Davis's death, Davis ★ Camp of Pittsburgh, Pennsylvania, issued a re-strike of this badge to be made of pewter with antiqued gold plate, a modern clutch pin, and black grosgrain ribbon. It is not hallmarked.

Secretary to the GAR Post:

By the 1920's, the ranks of GAR veterans were thinning. They turned to their Allied Orders (the WRC, SUVCW, LGAR, DUVCW, ASUVCW) to provide support. A pin bar was produced in bronze to match the membership badge and read, "Secretary•Post•GAR".

A second variation reads, "Secretary To Post". Many of these bars have been found with only the Post flag ribbon attached, but they could also be attached to the membership badge of the wearer. These pin bars were produced by Joseph Davison, of Philadelphia, Pennsylvania. The Sons' Committee on Rules and Regulations adopted this on Sept. 15, 1927:

"Be it enacted, that Posts in the several Departments may admit the Sons of Veterans at their option, to meetings of said Posts, but not to participate in any of the proceedings by vote or otherwise. They can be engaged by the Posts to act as Secretary if so desired" Small Bar Pin marked "Sec'y GAR Post" will be furnished. CDR Stowits, Quartermaster General, GAR."[129]

Secretary to Department GAR.

A pin bar was produced in silver with the words "GAR Department Secretary". It is usually found with Department red edged flag ribbon only. It was produced by Joseph Davison Company of Philadelphia, Pennsylvania.

Secretary to the National GAR.

A pin bar was produced in gold with the words "GAR National Secretary" with gold edged GAR flag ribbon. Only two persons held this office: Katherine Flood and Cora Gillis. Both were past National Presidents of the Daughters of Union Veterans of the Civil War and served much as an Executive Director would today.

They were paid employees of the GAR. It is not illustrated.

Sons of Veterans Twenty-Five Year Bar.

It was manufactured by Charles Robbins Company of Attleboro, Massachusetts.

Silver Numeral Pins

These are silver plated numbers to be worn on the member badge to indicate years of continuous membership. The following silver numerals are available 10, 25, 30, 35, 40, 45, 50, 55, 60, 65, 70, and 75. These numerals were manufactured by various jewelers. None are hallmarked.

SUVCW Miniature Badges

Miniature badges are scale replicas of full size badges and are designed to be worn on formal evening attire. They are available with Camp, Department, or National ribbons. A small star attachment was authorized for meritorious service. Also a small palm leaf attachment was authorized for combat veteran.

Type I. This miniature badge has a bronze finish pendant with hidden pin back. There is no hallmark. Made by Dondero Company, Washington, D.C.

Type II. This miniature badge has brown antiquing on a brass pendant with hidden pin back. There is no hallmark. Made by Dondero Company, Washington, D.C. Not illustrated.

Type III. This miniature badge has black antiquing on a brass pendant. It is hallmarked "Dondero, Inc.". There is a hidden clutch pin mount on the back of the ribbon.

Type I Obverse   Type I Reverse

Type III Obverse

Type IV   Type IV
Obverse   Reverse

Type IV. This miniature badge has brown antiquing on a copper pendant. It is hallmarked with an "S" within a shield. There is a hidden clutch pin mount on the back of the ribbon. Camp, Department, and National ribbons were available. It is made and hallmarked by Simons Brothers.

Type V. Beginning in January 2014, all badges are being manufactured by ESCO of Milwaukee, Wisconsin. The correct hallmark "ESCO Milwaukee" appears on the bottom of the reverse of the pendant. Not illustrated.

In 2010, the National Organization authorized the addition of the following miniature badges:

SUVCW Miniature Past Camp Commander Badge and SUVCW Miniature Past Department Commander Badge

This miniature badge is a one inch silver finished iron cross pendant with a Camp, half inch wide, ribbon. It is hallmarked with an "S" within a shield. There is a hidden clutch pin mount on the back of the ribbon. It is made by Simons Brothers.

This miniature badge is a one inch silver cross pendant with red and white enamel, a blue center, with a Department half-inch wide ribbon. It is hallmarked with an "S" within a shield. There is a hidden clutch pin mount on the back of the ribbon. It is also made by Simons Brothers.

Past Camp   Past Dept.
Commander   Commander

SUVCW Miniature Past Commander-in-Chief Badge

This badge is a miniature Gold Star pendant with a red enamel center and a National half-inch wide ribbon. It is hallmarked with an "S" within a shield. It has a hidden clutch pin mount on the back of the ribbon. It was made by Simons Brothers in 2012 and 2013. Beginning in January 2014, all badges are being manufactured by ESCO of Milwaukee, Wisconsin.

Miniature SVR Badge

This miniature badge is a three-fourths inch circular copper finished pendant with the Sons of Veterans Reserve eagle. The words "Sons of Veterans Reserve 1903" surround the eagle. It has a red, white, and blue striped half-inch wide ribbon and no hallmark. There is a hidden clutch pin mount on the back of the ribbon. It was made by Hermann Werks, Hermann, Missouri, and is not hallmarked.

SUVCW Miniature Military Service Badge

This miniature badge is a one inch silver round pendant featuring an eagle atop a federal shield. The words "Sons of Union Veterans of the Civil War" surround the eagle design. It is suspended by a half inch wide Department ribbon. It was made by Simons Brothers and is hallmarked with an "S" within a shield. There is a hidden clutch pin mount on the back of the ribbon.

Beginning in January 2014, all badges are being manufactured by ESCO of Milwaukee, Wisconsin. The correct hallmark "ESCO Milwaukee" appears on the bottom of the reverse of the pendant.

SUVCW Miniature War Service Badge

A miniature bronze cross badge was illegally created overseas and sold outside of the organization. It was never approved by nor sold by the Sons' Order. Not illustrated.

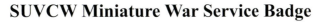

SUVCW Camp Commander's Badge

In order to recognize the Camp Commander, a silver plated badge was authorized in 1989. The badge is passed on to his successor each year.

Type I. A **Type XIX** Sons' badge silver plated with a matte finish pendant and bar. The top bar reads "Sons of Union Veterans of the Civil War". It was produced by Simons Brothers.

Type II. Beginning in January 2014, all badges are being manufactured by Erffmeyer and Son Company of Milwaukee, Wisconsin. They are hallmarked on the reverse "ESCO Milwaukee."

SUVCW Department Commander's Badge

Approved in 1947, this badge is worn while serving as Department Commander. It is passed on to his successor each year.

Type I. This design is adapted from a **Type XVIII** Sons' badge in bronze finish with a secondary bar reading "Department Commander". A red Department ribbon is used. It was manufactured by and has the hallmark of, "August Frank, Philadelphia, Pennsylvania." It is not illustrated.

Type II. The design is adapted from a **Type XIX** Sons' badge, but has a gold plated pin bar, pendant, and a secondary bar that reads, "Department Commander". A red Department ribbon is used. It was made by Simons Brothers and has their hallmark of an "S" in a shield on the pin bar.

Type III. Beginning in January 2014, all badges are being manufactured by Erffmeyer and Son Company of Milwaukee, Wisconsin. They are hallmarked on the reverse "ESCO Milwaukee."

SUVCW ROTC Badges

Authorized by the Sons of Union Veterans in 2002 for a Camp to present to ROTC and Junior ROTC cadets.

Type I. A silver colored shield shaped badge with the Sons' Coat of Arms on the obverse. Ribbon is the blue Sons membership ribbon. Type I was discontinued because the ribbon was identical to the Military Officers Association of America (formerly known as The Retired Officers Association). The Air Force ROTC had quit using the SUVCW medal for their awards program because of the same ribbon pattern as MOAA. To keep this award in all branches of ROTC and JROTC **type II** was introduced in 2006.

Type II. A copper colored shield shaped badge with the Sons' Coat of Arms on the obverse. Ribbon is white background with two blue stripes on the left edge and two red stripes on the right. The badge is imported and not hallmarked.

Matching military ribbon for uniform wear is included with the badge.

SUVCW Life Member Bar

From the earliest days of the Order, the national organization bestowed constitutional life memberships upon our founders. In 1956, our Congressional charter allowed members to purchase Life Membership with the lump sum payment invested and the interest paying the member's dues for life. In order to recognize those men who paid for a lifetime membership, a gold bar reading, "Life Member" was approved in 1958. There are two types of bars issued.

Type I. A gold bar one and one-fourth inch wide (the same width as the ribbon), by one-fourth inch high with two prongs on the back to be pushed through the ribbon and bend in the back. This style was issued from 1958 until approximately 1990 when stock was exhausted. These were manufactured by August C. Frank Company of Philadelphia, Pennsylvania.

Type II. A three-fourths inch gold bar with black letters. Single clutch pin on back. It was made by Simons Brothers. After January 2014, it is manufactured by ESCO of Milwaukee, Wisconsin, and it is not hallmarked.

SUVCW Real Son Bar

In 2011, a three-fourths inch gold bar with black letters reading "Real Son" was issued for attachment to the membership badge of actual Sons of Union Veterans. It had a single clutch pin attachment. Not illustrated.

SV - SUVCW Lapel Buttons & Recognition Pins

Type IIa Obverse Type IIa Reverse Type IIb Reverse Type IIIa Obverse Type IVa Obverse

Type I. A tricolor bar (1882) about three-fourths inch long, made of red, white, & blue silk, was the first recognition pin. Not illustrated.

Type IIa. Recognition bronze button (1887) shield shaped with crossed swords and wreath. Bailey, Banks, and Biddle was the official jeweler at this time.

Type IIb. Recognition bronze pin (1887) same design with pin attachment.

Type IIIa. Recognition button with full color cloisonne (1887).

Type IIIb. Recognition button (1887) with pin attachment.

Type IIIc. Enameled full color shield shaped button modified as stickpin, etc.

Type IVa. Recognition button in oxidized silver (1887) same design.

Type IVb. Recognition pin in oxidized silver (1887) same design with pin attachment.

Type IVc. Recognition pin in oxidized silver (1887 design) attached to a stick pin for men's ties.

Type IIIc & IVc Reverse

| Type Va | Type Vb | Type VI | Type VII |
| Obverse | Obverse | Obverse | Obverse |

Type Va. Regulation cloisonné recognition button (1891) a half inch round "SV" in red and white enamel in center rays emanating outward in gold metallic, with a blue transparent enamel around the outer edge and the words "Sons of Veterans". It has a smooth back hallmarked Robbins.

Type Vb. Regulation cloisonné recognition button (1891) five-eighths inch in diameter. Similar in design to **Type Va**; however, the reverse has a cook pot over a campfire design. Joseph Davison was the manufacturer and it is not hallmarked.

Type VI. Regulation enameled button - one-half inch in diameter. "SV" in blue and white cloisonné in center, with rays emanating outward in gold metallic. A red transparent cloisonné with "Rhode Island Div S of V Get One Club" around the outer edge. Some have a smooth back with no hallmark, others have been found hallmarked "Wm. Brown Co. Providence, RI".

Type VII. Regulation hard stamped enamel recognition button (1915) a half inch round "SV" in red & white enamel in center rays emanating outward in gold metallic, blue enamel around outer edge and words "Sons of Veterans". The smooth back has a screw post. It is hallmarked "CM Robbins".

Type VIII
Obverse

Type VIII. A recognition button consisting of a miniature badge pendant with "SV" with a solid post construction and hallmarked " Charles Robbins Co."

Type VIX. A recognition button consisting of a miniature badge pendant with "SV" with a solid post construction with no hallmark.

Type X. A recognition button consisting of a miniature badge pendant with "SV" with a screw post construction with no hallmark.

Type XI Obverse   Type XI Reverse

Type XI. A recognition button consisting of a miniature badge pendant with "SUV" with a screw post construction and no hallmark, circa 1926.

Type XII. A recognition button consisting of a miniature badge pendant with "SUV" with a screw post construction and no hallmark, but was made by August Frank 1940-1950s.

Type XII
Obverse

Type XIII
Obverse

Type XIII. A recognition button consisting of a miniature badge pendant with "SUV" and a clutch pin backing. It has no hallmark, but was made by August Frank 1960-1970s.

Type XIV. A Tie tack of a miniature badge pendant with "SUV" in the center of an eagle. Polished bronze with chain and tie tack back. It is manufactured by Klitner Company of Providence, Rhode Island. Not Illustrated.

Type XV. A miniature badge pendant with "SUV" on eagles breast with a clutch pin backing. It has the hallmark "S" in a shield. It was made by Simon Brothers, circa 1987-2013. Not Illustrated.

Type XVI. Beginning in January 2014, lapel pins will be manufactured by Erffmeyer and Sons of Milwaukee, Wisconsin. Not Illustrated.

Past Camp Commander's Lapel Button

Sons of Union Veteran Iron Cross pendant approximately one-half inch worn as a tie tack or a lapel pin. Made of silver colored material, it was sold by Sons Charitable Foundation in 2011. Imported with no hallmark.

Past Division / Department Commander's Lapel Button

Type I. Sons of Veterans Silver Cross pendant approximately one-half inch in diameter was worn as a lapel button and made of sterling silver and enamel. Not hallmarked. Either Joseph Davison or Charles Robbins was probably the manufacturer

Type II. Sons of Union Veterans Silver Cross pendant three-fourths of an inch in diameter and worn as a tie tack. It was sold by the Sons Charitable Foundation in 2011. It is made of a silver colored material with no hallmark as it is imported.

Past Commander-in-Chief's Lapel Button

(Courtesy of
Chester Shriver)

Past Commander-in-Chief star approximately one-half inch in diameter made of gold and worn as a lapel button. These were individually handcrafted with the badge. It was usually presented as a testimonial gift from the Past Commanders-in-Chief to the out-going Commander-in-chief. Not hallmarked, but made by I. Bedichimer of Philadelphia.

Miniature Enameled Badge Lapel Pin:

Type I Obverse

Type I. A miniature members badge with enameled camp ribbon. Imported with no hallmark. Sold by Sons Charitable Foundation.

Type II. A miniature members badge with enameled Department red ribbon. Imported with no hallmark. Sold by Sons Charitable Foundation.

Type II Obverse

Type III Obverse   Type IV Obverse   Type V Obverse

Type III. A miniature members badge with enameled National organization ribbon. Imported with no hallmark. Sold by Sons Charitable Foundation.

Type IV. A miniature Past Camp Commander's badge with enameled Camp ribbon. Imported with no hallmark. Sold by Sons Charitable Foundation.

Type V. A miniature Past Department Commander's badge with enameled Department ribbon. Imported with no hallmark. Sold by Sons Charitable Foundation.

These miniature badges were sold as a fund-raiser by the Sons Charitable Foundation beginning in 2004.

Department Lapel Pins

Various Divisions and Departments identified their members with custom-made lapel pins. Here is an example from the Maine Division. Not hallmarked.

SVR Lapel Button

A five-eighths inch round lapel button. It is a copper color with the SVR eagle as the central motif. The lettering around edge reads: "Sons of Veterans Reserve * 1903". It has a single clutch pin on the back with no hallmark. Imported and sold by the Sons Charitable Foundation 2013.

 152

Souvenir Lapel Pins - numerous designs may exist.

SV initials in the Sears, Roebuck & Co 1892 catalog #61593 and sold for $1.10 each.

SV initials with gold bar.

SV miniature badge - Made in the 1890s by various jewelers in gold plate; they sold for $1.00 each.

SV badge pendant in gold and enamel.

SV shield in gold with engraved "SV" made by the Bainbridge Company of Syracuse, New York. This design was in the Bainbridge catalog for a number of different men's and women's lodges between 1875 and 1900.

Rosette

An additional buttonhole decoration was authorized in 1912 consisting of a silk rosette.

A red, white, and blue rosette not to exceed five-eighths inch in diameter. The central circular disk to be divided into four segments more than half the area being devoted to opposed segments of blue alternating with white; the band is to be composed of alternating red and white.[130] Most hereditary orders have official rosettes; but due to their silk material they tend to soil and are less popular than the metal buttonhole decorations.

Type I. Rosette design is as described. These were manufactured by Bailey, Banks, and Biddle from 1912-1916, and discontinued when supplies were exhausted. The post and back are permanently affixed. Not illustrated.

Type II. The rosette design is the same as **Type I** and manufactured by Dexter Rosettes. Today, they have a clutch pin backing as men's suits rarely have buttonholes.

SV / SUVCW Silk Memorial and Camp Ribbons

As with the GAR and the other Allied Orders, black silk Memorial Ribbons were worn for Memorial Day and funerals of Comrades or Brothers. Red, White, and Blue ribbons might be worn at picnics, Fourth of July parades, etc. These ribbons usually feature the name of the Camp, the location, and a picture of a badge or patriotic design.

SV / SUVCW Encampment Ribbons

These ribbons usually feature the dates of the convention and are made of red silk ribbons for Department Encampments and gold silk ribbons for attendance at the National Encampment. Examples in other colors such as red, white, and blue, solid blue and black exist as well as other fabrics.

Lafayette Camp 140 of Manhattan, NY

Both the Grand Army Post and the Sons Camp bore the same name and number. The Sons Camp was organized in 1887 and had a number of prominent Sons including descendants of Grant, Sherman, Sickles, and McClellan.

Due to their location, they were large in numbers and financially successful. The Camp surrendered its charter and $25,000 in cash in 1975 on the condition that all surviving members be given life memberships and their camp number would never be issued again.

NY Camp 140
Rosette

The Lafayette Camp issued a gold and red enameled badge to its members. In 1919, the cost of this badge was $10.00 and the camp rosette an additional twenty-five cents. The Grand Army post badge is featured under post badges on page 98 and had a Grand Army star in the center rather than the Sons insignia.

John A. Koltes Camp 171 of Brooklyn, NY

Founded on December 5, 1882 as a chapter of the Post System, it was known as Koltes Post # 17. It merged into the Camp System March 12, 1891. It was fully armed as Troop F and equipped as cavalry. More than 400 men served in this camp. Being a wealthy camp they produced several insignia unique to their chapter.

The Ten Year Service Badge was a small bronze cross bearing the Camp System pendant in the center surrounded by the words "Koltes Camp No. 171 Org.1882" and "10 Years Service" on the pin bar attached by three links of chain to the pendant.

Gold Fifty year pin

A gold bar was issued to commemorate the camp's fiftieth anniversary. This bar pins onto the member's badge ribbon. It was gold plated one and one-fourths inches long by one-fourth inch high. It has blue lettering that reads, "1882 KOLTES CAMP 1932".

 156

A Sample of SV / SUVCW Encampment Badges

Encampment badges were issued from 1890 until the early 1930s. A ribbon with an elaborate pin bar was popular and more economical in the 1930s and 1940s. Plain printed ribbons were used by delegates from the 1950s until the mid-1990s when reasonably priced badges could be imported from overseas.

1891

1896

1901

1907

1914

1915

1922

1941

Sons Belt Buckles - A sampling

Coat of Arms Buckle. This Camp system buckle features a soldier and sailor on either side of a shield. It is usually found as a rough casting approximately two inches by three inches. This coat of arms design was patented by Major A. P. Davis in 1887.

Mills style SV Belt Buckle. This buckle was used with the three inch wide military web belts that held cartridges. This buckle dates from the Spanish-American War era circa 1898.

The SVR Oval Buckle is stamped brass with the back filled with lead similar to the U.S. buckles of the Civil War. This buckle was authorized as an enlisted man's buckle. This same design has also been found as a cartridge box plate with two loops on the reverse. Circa 1905 to 1940s.

The SUV Oval Buckle is solid brass two inches by three inches, with, "Sons of Union Veterans of the Civil War" and "Fraternity, Charity and Loyalty" around edge with the badge pendant in center. Numbered and hallmarked on reverse "Anacortes Brass Works" and dated 2000.

A small polished brass buckle was issued with a navy web belt in 2011. It was one and seven-eights inches by one and three-eights inches and features a three-fourth inch badge pendant.

SV Coat of Arms Brass Buttons

Domed brass button with full coat of arms, a soldier and a sailor, with the words "Filii Veteranorum". The reverse reads, "Pat'd A. P. Davis, Pittsburgh". In the past this has been mistakenly identified as a Post System button from New York, but it is clearly from the Pittsburgh Camp System. Two sizes were issued: one inch coat buttons and one-half inch cuff or vest buttons. Major Davis sold these at $7.50 gross to the Sons organization for uniform use, circa 1887-1920.

Field Day Lithograph Buttons

Souvenirs issued to participants in inter-company competitions and camp inspections. Most examples date prior to World War I and issued by the Pennsylvania Brigade.

Metal and Embroidery Hat Wreath

Type I.   SVG hat wreath worn by commissioned officers of the Sons of Veterans Guards; in use from 1893 to 1894. An example was not found, but it is listed in regulations. It is not illustrated.

| Type IIa | Type IIb | Type III |

Type IIa. SV hat wreath worn by uniformed Sons of Veterans members.

Type IIb. SV hat wreath with camp numerals worn by uniformed Sons of Veterans members.

Type III. SUV hat wreath usually worn by Department or Camp officers and by members and Camp Guards not assigned under the SVR.

| Type IV | Type Va | Type Vc |

Type IV. Embroidered wreaths for use by SUV members on their kepis. The various manufacturers had slight variations of the design in both cotton and gold bullion thread.

Type Va. SVR hat wreath. Brass with gold finish worn by SVR Commissioned Officers. Not hallmarked, but made by Gemsco, Milford, Connecticut, in the 1970s.

Type Vb. SVR hat wreath silver letters "SVR" within gold wreath worn by SVR commissioned officers in the 1970s and later. Not illustrated.

Type Vc. Embroidered wreath with letters SVR within. Worn by commissioned SVR officers. Various suppliers including the Sons Charitable Foundation.

Circular SVR Hat Devise

Another variation of a SVR Hat Device is a one and one-half inch diameter bronze circular badge featuring the SVR eagle on front and a screw post on back. No manufacturer mark, but probably made by Joseph Davison. It was used in 1920s, during that period when ranks were indicated by circular discs and diamonds. No example was located for this publication, but the description appears in SVR regulations of the period. Not illustrated.

Enlisted Men Crossed Arms of Service Hat Insignia

Arms of Service Hat Device: Crossed Muskets or Rifles, Crossed Cannons, or Crossed Swords. These usually have the unit number attached on top and "SV" attached on bottom. It was worn by "armed" SV units in the 1880s and 1890s and SVR units after 1903.

Pennsylvania Brigade units may also have a red enameled keystone centered on crossed arms.

Collar Insignia

Collar insignia - for SVG The letters may either be embroidered or brass (1892-1893). No example has been located.

SV collar insignia was in use from 1882 to 1903.

SVR collar brass- 1904 to 1930s

All officers were to wear a collar insignia described as "a coat of arms of the United States of bronze metal (matte gold color), with the following modifications: The shield on the breast of the eagle shall bear a monogram composed of the letters, in bold relief, S.V. and R.; the sunburst will be replaced by a scroll rising from the eagle's beak, bearing the words 'Filii Veteranorum.' To be worn on the collar, one inch from the end." [131]   All officers were instructed to wear the 1903 US Army regulation collar insignia in addition to the SVR eagle.

| Type I | Type II | Type III |

Type I. Solid Brass "SVR" eagle as described above. Not hallmarked.

Type II. Solid Brass "SVR" eagle as described above. Letters "SVR" enameled in red, white, and blue on solid brass eagle as above. Not hallmarked.

Type III. A reproduction of the earlier **Type II** SVR insignia was re-issued in 2012 by the Sons Charitable Foundation. It has a shiny gold finish with transparent red and blue enamel. As it is imported it is not hallmarked.

SVR Collar Insignia 1940- present.[132]

For use by enlisted men on the field uniform, a round one inch polished brass disc with the letters "SVR". These were manufactured by Gemsco, Milford, Connecticut. It was used in the 1940s to the early 1960s.

Commissioned Officers wore the cut out letters "SVR" in polished brass with gold plating, about one and one-fourth inch long, on their collars.   Insignia from the 1940s and 1950s have screwposts on the back. Ones from the 1960s and 1990s have a clutch backing on a smooth pin.

1940s Obverse and Reverse   1960s Obverse   1990s Obverse
                                                          Current

Diamonds and Disc Rank Insignia

Pennsylvania Brigade Regulations dated February 25, 1929 reads:

For officers: "Rank insignia shall be of the design authorized by the War Department for all military organizations other than those in the US service, described as follows:

(a) Second Lieutenant – one silver disc

(b) First Lieutenant – two silver disc

(c) Captain – three silver disc

(d) Major – one gold diamond

(e) Lieutenant Colonel – two gold diamonds

(f) Colonel – three gold diamonds

"All officers of the Department Staff shall wear gold rank insignia. These devices to be worn according to the regulations of the US Army, on the shoulder tabs of the service uniforms. The Department device shall be the keystone."[133]

Division and Department Hat Insignia "Corps Badges"[134]

These Division or Department emblems were used by the Sons from their earliest military training days and continued as Sons of Veterans Reserve emblems after the general membership became a fraternal lodge without military uniforms. In recent years, several Departments have re-adopted their Department Corps emblems for use on their kepis.

This list is from 1887 except Florida:

Alabama & Tennessee: an acorn

California – crescent

Connecticut – a tre-foil

Florida - (Adopted in 2012)

Michigan – a crescent & Star

Illinois – a quinque foil

Connecticut

Florida

Michigan

Illinois

Indiana –

Iowa – a dove

Kansas – a sunflower

Maine – a Greek cross

Minnesota – a Maltese Cross

Missouri – Hexagon with arrow & MO

Montana – Sword & Arrow

Nebraska – ear of corn

New Hampshire – Shield with NH

New Jersey – a diamond

New York – fan leaved cross

 Ohio – a star

Pennsylvania – a keystone

Rhode Island – Shield with Anchor

Vermont – Geneva Cross

West Virginia – Heart

Indiana   Iowa

Missouri   New Jersey

New York   Ohio

Pennsylvania   Vermont

Most designs were made in red with a gold border for dress uniform; and of bronze for field service uniform.

Meritorious Service Bar Ribbon 1960-1975

One and one-fourth inch wide overall ribbon for military uniform wear. This is divided into 5 mm red, 4 mm white, 15 mm blue, 4 mm white, and 5 mm red. It has a clutch pin back.

Meritorious Service Badges 1999 to present:

One and one-fourth inch round pendant with SVR eagle surrounded by the words "Sons of Veterans Reserve • 1881". Back left blank for engraving. Ribbon is vertical stripe in red, white, blue, and old gold. Hidden pin bar on the reverse. These were manufactured and hallmarked by Esco, Milwaukee, Wisconsin.

Type I. Designed as described above but silver plated. These were for District use. Not illustrated.

Type II. Designed as above but gold plated. These were used by the National Military Departments. Hallmarked, "ESCO".

Type II
(Courtesy of Gordon R. Bury)

Recruiting Bar Ribbon 1960-1975

This military ribbon bar is designed to be worn on a military uniform. It is like the modern military wear with clutch pins on back. There is no corresponding badge. The bar is one and one-fourth inch wide and consists of three segments: the left one third is green, the center one third is yellow, and the right one third is green. This ribbon bar is awarded for recruiting a new member into the Sons of Veterans Reserve.

Recruiting Ribbon

Exceptional Service Bar Ribbon 1960-1975

This military ribbon bar is designed to be worn on a military uniform. It is like the modern military wear with clutch pins on back. There is no corresponding medal. The ribbon is one and one-fourth inch wide and consists of three segments: the left 9 mm blue, 12 mm old gold, and 9 mm blue on the right.

Exceptional Service Award
Ribbon

SVR Membership Badge

This badge has a red, white, and blue striped ribbon with no visible bar pin. There is a one inch round pendant with SVR eagle surrounded by words "Sons of Veterans Reserve •1903". It is hallmarked on the reverse "Esco•Milwaukee". This badge was first issued in 1998.

Type I. Design as above, made with a copper finish and sold to members. Two hundred badges were made in 1998.

Type II. Design as above but made with a silver finish and issued as a badge for District Commanders. It is passed on to succeeding District Commanders. Ten badges were made in 1998. Not illustrated.

Type III. Design as above, but gold plated. This badge was issued to the National Commanding Officer and then passed on to succeeding Commanding Officers. Two badges were manufactured in 1998. Not illustrated.

SVR Centennial Badge

Heavy antique bronze shield shaped pendant two and one-half inches high by two inches wide. Obverse: SVR logo in center, with the words "Sons of Veterans Reserve" above the logo and "100 years of Service" below. A scroll beneath the shield reads "1903 2003". Reverse reads "Sons of Veterans Reserve Centennial 1903 to 2003". It has a hidden pin bar and a one and one-quater inch ribbon in royal blue and gold. There is no hallmark, but it was manufactured by Hermann Werks of Hermann, Missouri.

(Courtesy of Keith Harrison)

SVR Past Commanding Officer's Badge

Authorized by the National Encampment in 2007 to honor Past Commanding Officers of the National Military Department, SVR.

Four of these badges have been issued as of 2014. Keith Harrison and David V. Medert received their's in life, while Chester Shriver and Charles Corfman were awarded their medals posthumously. Brother Harrison is the only member to have served as Commanding Officer, National Military Department, SVR, and Commander-in-Chief of both the Sons and the Loyal Legion.

Pennsylvania Brigade, SVR

The Pennsylvania Brigade of the Sons of Veterans Reserve was the largest of the SVR units and the most active. For this reason, a number of badges, pins, and mementos exist. There are a number of paper commissions and membership cards that can be found as well.

Field Service Badge

A large chocolate bronze keystone featuring the SVR Eagle surrounded by words "Pennsylvania Brigade". The pin bar that is attached by chain links reads "Field Service". It is not hallmarked and made by Joseph Davison.

In 1917, the bronze keystone pendant of the Field Service Badge was replaced with a silver or gold pendant for Meritorious Service. Not hallmarked and made by Joseph Davison.

Meritorious Service Award

A gold edged, red enameled keystone, with SVR eagle in gold, and "SVR" in red, white, and blue letters on a black shield over the eagle's breast. The words, "Penna. Brigade" are at the bottom. It has gold SVR service bars attached and is not hallmarked.

(Courtesy of Joe Mitrovich)

Annual Service Bars

A bronze bar was issued each year with the year and location of the annual encampment. A small keystone with "SVR" is in the center of the bar. These are not hallmarked and are made by Joseph Davison of Philadelphia.

Service Badge and Attendance Pins

A Service Badge was authorized in 1917 consisting of a bronze round pendant. Bronze bars are issued for one year's service, silver bars for every three year's service, and gold bars for every six year's service. Silver bars replacing bronze bars and gold bars replacing silver bars. These are not hallmarked.

 168

SVR National Encampment Badges

Beginning in 1970 through 1995, the Sons of Veterans Reserve hosted an annual reunion and encampment of Civil War reenactment troops. A commemorative badge, and sometimes an embroidered patch was produced and issued to all participants.

1970 - Lisbon, OH. – Features a US Mint, Lincoln 39mm bronze coin in a plastic case, marked "Lisbon 70".

1971 - Indianapolis, IN. – A one and one-fourth bronze pendant with the SVR Logo. 150th anniversary of Indianapolis with red, white, and blue stripe ribbon.

1972 - Lancaster, OH. – An Ohio shaped copper pendant approximately one and three-fourths inches by two inches featuring the William T. Sherman bust on obverse with a white ribbon.

1973 - Gettysburg, PA. – A copper one and one-fourth inch pendant with the SVR logo. 110th anniversary of Gettysburg with a dark blue ribbon.

1974 - Ft Wayne, IN.

1975 - Ravenna, OH. – A one and one-quarter inch brass dome with the US Coat of Arms. It is hand stamped "6th SVR Natl." It has a three-fourths inch red, white, and blue ribbon.

1976 - Port Jervis, NJ.

1977 - Gahanna, OH. – A one and one-half inch bronze pendant with the SVR logo and a white ribbon.

1978 - Geneva, NY. – The gray enameled pendant looks like a Minnie Bullet with a dark blue ribbon.

1979 - Location Unknown.

1980 - Location Unknown.

1981 - Gettysburg, PA. – A one and one-half inch copper pendant with the SVR logo and Sons blue membership ribbon.

 169

1982 - Perrysville, KY. – A one and one-half inch antiqued silver pendant SVR logo with a blue and gray ribbon.

1983 - Branchport, NY. – A one and one-fourth inch red enameled Maltese cross pendant with a gold ribbon.

1984 - none held.

1985 - Delaware City, DE. – A one and one-half inch antiqued gold pendant with the SVR logo and a red ribbon.

SVR Encampments were sporadically held for the next ten years until 1995.

Western Spring 2001 Badge

This badge was issued for a joint Sons of Union Veterans and Sons of Confederate Veterans memorial involving the interment of an unknown soldier's remains, located on Missionary Ridge, Chattanooga, Tennessee.

Reverse   Obverse

 170

Iron Brigade Cross Badge

Issued by LTC. Ernest von Frankenberg, SVR in 1971 for ten years service in one of the reactivated Iron Brigade regiments. Five armed cross identifies the five Iron Brigade regiments with "SUV" in the center. Only 25 badges were struck. They were issued in bronze, but could be silver plated for 20 years and gold plated for 30 years service. They are hallmarked "Esco".

Type I. Is a full size bronze badge with no visible pin bar.

Type II. Is a miniature badge with no pin bar.

SVR Unit Citation 2010

SVR Units may be awarded a unit citation for being exceptionally meritorious in promoting the goals and objectives of the Sons or the SVR. Individual members are awarded a **Type I** pin.

Type I. A white enamel oval pin bearing the SVR eagle logo and two branches of leaves on the obverse. Approximately one and one-half inches high by two and one-half inches wide. It has a clutch pin attachment and is not illustrated.

Blazer Patches

Patches for use on men's jackets and blazers have been offered through the years as a fund-raiser for the National Organization or various Departments. Patches have consisted of the badge pendant or the coat of arms and this is offered in either a colored or a metallic gold embroidery. This brown and gold patch was an incentive for the National Patriotic Instructor's Fund in 1970. The metallic gold patch is available in 2014 from the Department of Michigan.

Uniform Patches

Local Camps often wore a uniform patch on the left shoulder of their uniforms as shown on the left. In the 1930s and 1940s, uniform patches were worn by SVR units like the First Connecticut Regiment shown on the right and by the Pennsylvania Brigade which is not illustrated.

Civil War Centennial Badges and Patches

Throughout the Civil WarCentennial of 1961 to 1965 a number of communities hosted local reenactment battles and issued commemorative badges, some with illustrations of GAR badges. While these Centennial badges are not official Sons badges, they are often found with SVR items from that era.

The design of the GAR badge is in the public domain so is no longer protected by copyright; it appeared on a number of Centennial items and reenactment badges and coins from 1961 through 1965 and later.

From 1966 to the mid-1970s, a reenactment organization headquartered in Maryland called itself "The GAR" or "Grand Armies of the Reunion". It had nothing to do with the Grand Army of the Republic or the GAR Allied Orders.

The Buckeye Blues Brigade, SVR from Ohio, had a jacket patch shaped like the Ohio state flag and was issued in the early 1960s. All Civil War Centennial patches were souvenirs and were not intended for uniform use.

Civil War Sesquicentennial Badges and Patches

In recognition of the 150th anniversary of the Civil War a number of commemorative badges and patches are likely to be issued from 2011 through 2015. The Sons issued an official sesquicentennial badge of the Civil War. Stars are attached to the ribbon: a bronze star for attending five sesquicentennial events, a silver star for ten events, and a gold star for fifteen events.

The medal is an oval bronze pendant with a tab. Inscribed on the medal are the words: "Sesquicentennial 150 American Civil War, 1861-1865 and, 2011-2015, Sons of Union Veterans of the Civil War Signature Event." It has a red, white, and blue vertical striped ribbon with metallic gold thread between each color.

The pin bar features an eagle with spread wings holding crossed cannon, sword, and armament. A clutch pin is on the back.

Sesquicentennial badges were issued to commemorate the 150th anniversary of decisive battles.

Challenge Coins

Challenge Coins are believed to have begun among military units during World War II. Each member of a unit or squadron received a coin. One member would issue the challenge and all members were required to produce their identifying coin or buy a round of drinks. Their popularity spread to other branches of the government and civilian organizations. Many organizations and even businesses issue these 39 mm coins as souvenirs. At least a dozen different designs of coins have been issued as of 2014 by the Sons of Veterans Reserve, Sons of Union Veterans, and the Loyal Legion.

| Bronze Level | Silver Level | Gold Level | Gold Mini |

SUVCW Charitable Foundation

On March 8, 2003, the Sons of Union Veterans Charitable Foundation was organized in Sandusky, Ohio, to raise money for various preservation and restoration projects. They are tax exempt under Internal Revenue Service code 501 (c) 3. There are six levels of membership with badges for each. Membership is voluntary.

Lincoln Fellowship and Sentinel Badges

Type I. Bronze Level $250 donation required

Type II. Silver Level $500 donation required

Type III. Gold Level $1000 donation required

A miniature gold star shaped badge created by the Sons of Union Veterans Charitable Foundation for donors at the $1000 level. Imported.

Type IV. Bronze Sentinel $1250 donation required – not illustrated

Type V. Silver Sentinel $1500 donation required

Type VI. Gold Sentinel $2000 donation required- not illustrated

Dr. Mary Edwards Walker Award

In 2011, the Sons of Union Veterans created a new award to be presented for exceptional service to the Order by a female member of the Allied Orders. The one and one-fourth inch gold pendant features a frontal view of Dr. Mary Walker on the obverse, surrounded by the words: "Doctor Mary Edwards Walker Medal – SUVCW".

The reverse has the inscription: "Awarded in grateful appreciation for service to the Sons of Union Veterans of the Civil War". It is hallmarked "c.2011 SUVCW".

Type I. National award with a thirty inch gold neck ribbon.

Type II. Departments can award the same badge with a solid red neck ribbon.

Meeting of the Last Civil War Widows Badge

On July 1, 1997, the Sons of Union Veterans and the Sons of Confederate Veterans hosted a historic meeting in Gettysburg, Pa. of two of the last four living Civil War widows.[135]

The badge consisted of a one and one-half inch pendant made in .999 silver, with a blue and gray ribbon and no visible pin bar. The simple engraving reads: "Meeting of the widows July 1, 1997, Gettysburg, PA." and the names of Mrs. Alberta Martin and Mrs. Daisy Anderson and their husbands' identification. It was made by Heritage Specialties Co. of Fort Meade, Florida.

One hundred and thirty four badges were made. The widows and eight host committee members (4 SUVCW and 4 SCV) were each given one; 50 went to the Sons of Union Veterans, 50 to the Sons of Confederate Veterans, and 24 were retained by the manufacturer. It is rumored that the badges sent to the Sons of Confederate Veterans were destroyed. Thus, perhaps only 82 badges exist. There is no manufacturer's hallmark nor any markings to show that it was issued by the Sons of Union Veterans and the Sons of Confederate Veterans. It is only marked with the ".999 fine" silver content.

Ephemera

Sons' ephemera or printed-paper materials are unlimited. Photographs, stationery, membership certificates, officers commissions for both the Sons and the SVR, printed General Orders, Department and National proceedings, forms, and calling cards exist; and more are being be produced each year. Like the Grand Army, stationery, postcards, and visiting cards are especially popular.

Pennsylvania Brigade
SVR Field Days 1910

(Pictures courtesy of
C. LeRoy Stoudt)

Inconsistencies

Although there were official changes in ribbons and badge designs, individual members, as well as local and state organizations, continued to use stock on hand. The vertical red, white, and blue striped ribbon has been found in use as late as 1910 on printed forms as well as actual badges. The official blue ribbon edged in red, white, and blue has been found on **Type Ia** badges; the owner replacing the old ribbon when it became worn with the newer "official" ribbon. Embossed seals were even slower to change. Membership cards dating from the 1970s still bear the embossed camp seal that reads "Sons of Veterans, USA", the name changed in 1926, fifty years before the date on the card.

Splinter Organizations

Sons of Union Veterans 1861-1865 of Cincinnati, Ohio

Only one badge has been located and it may be a Past Commander's badge rather than a membership badge. The rectangular pin bar reads, "Fred H. Alms Commandery No. 1". The shield shaped pendant reads "Sons of Union Veterans 1861-1865" surrounding "SUV" with "October 11, 1907" on the bottom. Chain links connect the bar with the pendant. It is backed by a blue edged post flag ribbon and a red, white, and blue striped ribbon. No hallmark, but likely made by James Murdock. The example is inscribed: "Robert C Heinzmann, past commander".

Lapel button – A sterling silver shield shaped button, seven-eighths of an inch high, and hallmarked by James Murdock, Cincinnati.

Sons of the Grand Army of the Republic

Type I. A maltese cross, one inch by one inch, mounted on a stickpin. The badge is made of sterling silver and reads "S. of GAR 1870". There is no manufacturer's hallmark.

Type II. We know there were several different Sons of the GAR organizations at different times. Each was short lived, but while other badge designs existed I have not located any for this publication.

Type I

 177

Military Order of the Loyal Legion U.S. Membership Badges

The enameled badge for the Military Order of the Loyal Legion of the United States is different from any other badge we have described. Both the obverse and the reverse sides of the badge are fully enameled. The official description follows:

"Obverse. A cross of eight points, gold, cantoned with rays of gold, forming a star – its long diameter one and three-tenths inches, its short diameter eight-tenths of an inch. The cross enameled, azure, charged with a smaller cross on like proportions, enameled white and edged with gold. In the centre thereof, within a circle four-tenths of an inch in diameter, enameled gules, the National Eagle displayed in gold. On the circle, gold, one-tenth of an inch wide, in relievo, the motto, LEX REGIT ARMA TUENTUR.

"Reverse. The star as above described. In the centre thereof, within a circle four-tenths of an inch in diameter, enameled gules, two sabres in saltire, their point in base; surmounted by a fasces palewise, ensigned with the Phrygian Cap; environed in chief with an arch of thirteen stars; in base, a wreath of laurel; all of gold. On the circle, gold, one-tenth of an inch wide, in relievo, the legend M.O., Loyal Legion, U.S. – MDCCCLXV." [136]

There is a small gold ring between the ribbon and pendant engraved with the membership number of the original owner of that badge. The badges were made by Bailey, Banks, and Biddle, Jewelers of Philadelphia, Pennsylvania.

The badge pendant is suspended from a red, white, and blue watered silk ribbon. The predominant color indicated class of membership. The Loyal Legion describes their badge as an eight pointed star (rather than Cross) enameled in bright blue (azure) and white enamel, with rays of gold inserted between each arm of the star. In the center of the star, a gold American eagle was displayed on red transparent enamel, surrounded by the words in Latin "Lex Regit, Arma Tuentur" which translates as "Laws Rule, Arms Defend."

The reverse has the same blue and white eight pointed star with golden rays and the center motif on transparent red enamel consists of crossed sabers and a fasces surmounted by a Phrygian cap, over which is an arch of 13 stars. The words surrounding the motif are "M.O. Loyal Legion, U.S., MDCCCLXV" The member's number was engraved on the gold link between the pendant and the ribbon.[137]

The small gold ring between the enameled pendant and the ribbon was engraved with the first member's registration number. If his badge was inherited by a son, a second number would be engraved on the ring. For First Degree members, the ribbon was red silk with a blue and white vertical stripe on each side. Second and Third Degree members wore a blue silk ribbon with red and white vertical stripe on the edges.[138] Members voted in 1929 to eliminate the blue centered ribbon and use the red centered ribbon for all members to take effect on January 1, 1936.

Type III Obverse   Reverse Types I-IV   Type II Obverse

Type I. Badge as described above. A veteran member wore a dark red centered silk ribbon with a blue and white vertical stripe on each side.

Type II. Badge in the same design with blue silk centered ribbon with a red and white vertical stripe on each side of blue center. This variety was issued to Second Class hereditary Companions. The shades of blue in the center varies from light to deep medium blue.

For more than 140 years all badges were made by Bailey, Banks, and Biddle of Philadelphia. None were hallmarked. With the merger of Bailey, Banks, and Biddle in 2007, a new manufacturer was selected: City Pride Limited of Philadelphia. The badges are still not hallmarked.

Type IIIa. Beginning on January 1, 1935, with the transition from the original veteran members to hereditary members, all hereditary members wear a grosgrain ribbon with a red center and a blue and white vertical stripe on each side. The blue centered ribbon described previously was discontinued.[139]

Type III Obverse   Type IV Obverse

Type IIIb. In 2013, due to the expense of gold bullion, companions' membership badges are gold over bronze or on special order made in 14 kt gold.

Type IV. Today, all Associates wear a solid blue grosgrain ribbon.

The badges are to be worn on formal occasion on the left breast. The MOLLUS officers might wear their pendant from a neck ribbon in the same color as the badge with the pendant just below the Adam's apple.

Commemorative Badges

Unlike the GAR and Sons who issued numerous badges for every encampment, the Loyal Legion rarely issued any commemorative badges or souvenirs and if any were issued they were in very small quantities.

On April 15-17, 1890, a twenty-fifth anniversary celebration was held in Philadelphia. A commemorative badge features the Loyal Legion reverse of the coat of arms with flags. The reverse is inscribed around the outer rim with: "25th Anniversary of the Order of Loyal Legion". Inside a memorial wreath it reads: "Held at Phila Pa April 15-17 1890". According to their printed record about 200 companions attended this event.

For the seventy-fifth anniversary in 1940 an ashtray was issued rather than a badge.

Twenty-fifth anniversary badge issued in 1890.

To date, no examples have been found of a 1915 fiftieth anniversary commemorative badge or a 1965 centennial commemorative badge.

In 1987, an extremely small quantity of badges was issued to commemorate the bicentennial of the United States Constitution by the Pennsylvania Commandery. The medal is bronze color with a blue and gold vertical stripe ribbon.

Obverse: Liberty Bell with "1776" and "Phila" inscribed around the bell and on the outside rim the following: "Proclaim Liberty throughout the land unto the inhabitants thereof".

Reverse: M.O.L.LU.S.

US Constitution 1787-1987

1987 Constitution commemoration
(Courtesy of Keith Harrison)

 181

Cello buttons

A one inch cello button featuring an American flag was issued in 1897 for the eighth national convention.

Rosette

The rosette was designed for everyday wear and recognition. The silk rosette lapel recognition was originally made in France for Bailey, Banks, and Biddle Jewelers of Philadelphia, Pa. Rosettes and badges are not worn at the same time. [140]

Type Ia. A rosette approximately five-eights inches in diameter with a predominantly red silk center was for veteran members until 1935. The original rosettes had stripes of cut fabric and a solid post attached to a round black metal backing. After 1935 both veteran and hereditary members wore this rosette.

Type Ib. A similar rosette is worn today but the red, white, and blue are woven rather than cut cloth and it has a pin with a separate clutch back.

Type II. A rosette with a predominantly blue silk center with a white loop was worn by hereditary members until January 1, 1936, when it was eliminated. According to Past Commander-in-Chief William Duval, the remaining stock was used in the 1950s to 1980s as the Commander-in-Chief and Past Commander-in-Chief Rosette.

Type III. A miniature rosette in the same colors as the hereditary members, but approximately one-fourth inch in diameter, is used for associate and honorary members.

Type IV. A miniature rosette with a silver ribbon behind it indicates Past State Commanders and Commandery-in-Chief officers.

Type V. A miniature rosette with a gold ribbon behind it is worn by a Commander-in-Chief or Past Commander–in-Chief.

Type VI. A rosette set in a gold wreath for life members was authorized in the 2010 bylaws, but was never issued.

Miniature Badges

Type I. A miniature badge with red centered, red, white, and blue ribbon was issued for original veteran companions and hereditary members.

Type II. A miniature badge with a solid blue ribbon was issued for associate members.

War Service Badge

Type I. In 1991 a buckle company produced and donated to MOLLUS one hundred war service badges. The Commandery-in-Chief considered the gift, but decided against the issuance of a War Service Badge. Since one hundred had been made, they were sold for $10.00 each to any member desiring it as a souvenir and the money placed in the treasury. MOLLUS officially still has no war service badge. Example shown is an artist rendering.

Type II. A miniature of the MOLLUS War Service badge (see above). It was never issued by MOLLUS.

State Commanders and Commander-in-Chief's Badge

MOLLUS State Commander's Jewel was made by Tiffany Jeweler, New York, and consists of a pocket emblem approximately two and one-half inches by two and one-half inches. There is no ribbon. On formal wear, it may be worn with a three inch wide red, white, and blue sash. This badge is passed on to his successor each year. The Commander–in-Chief jewel was also made by Tiffany Jewelers and is approximately three inches by three inches in size.

MOLLUS ROTC Badge

Type I. College ROTC Award: A one and one-fourth inch round bronze pendant with crossed sabers in the background, fasces in the middle ground and an American eagle with open wings in the front surround by the motto: Lex Rehit Arma Tuentur. The reverse has a blank space for engraving. It was manufactured by Bailey, Banks, and Biddle, but not hallmarked. It uses the regulation membership ribbon with red center and no visible pin bar.

Type II. This ROTC badge is of the same design as **Type I**, except it is in a shiny gold finish. It has clutch pins on the reverse. The badge is manufactured by City Pride LTD. of Philadelphia, and is not hallmarked.

A matching one and one-fourth inch service bar made of regulation ribbon is included to wear on military uniforms.

Special Achievement Merit and Distinguished Service Award

The Special Achievement Merit badge on the left is the same design as the college ROTC badge except it is manufactured in antique brass with a red, white, and blue striped ribbon with no visible pin bar. They are made by Bailey, Banks, and Biddle and are not hallmarked.

The Distinguished Service Award badge on the right is the also the same design as the college ROTC badge except it is in silver plate. It uses a red membership ribbon with no visible pin bar. It is made by Bailey, Banks, and Biddle and are not hallmarked.

Loyal Legion Blazer Patch

A gold bullion embroidery patch made to wear on the left pocket of a man's jacket.

MOLLUS BUTTONS

These gold plated buttons feature an embossed eagle design and were made for use on a man's jacket. They are available in both jacket and cuff button size. They were manufactured by and hallmarked on reverse, "Ben Silver Charleston, SC."

MOLLUS Recruiting Badge

This badge features Abraham Lincoln on the obverse. The reverse reads "MOLLUS Recruiting Award". It is awarded to members recruiting three new hereditary members. Small stars attached to the ribbon indicate multiple awards. Originally manufactured by Bailey, Banks, and Biddle, it was issued with a purplish blue satin ribbon. Today it features a similar design with a dark blue grosgrain ribbon and is manufactured by City Pride LTD.

MOLLUS Challenge Coin

Challenge coins are being released by Past Commanders-in-Chief and various State commanderies.

MOLLUS Ephemera

In 1890, John Philip Sousa released the *Loyal Legion March* for MOLLUS's twenty-fifth anniversary.

In 1992, seventy-two volumes of war papers were reprinted by Broadfoot Publishing Company.

An index to the War Papers are available on the world wide web at:

http://www.suvcw.org/mollus/war/warpapers.htm

The Grand Army Death Badge and other Fantasies

All researchers, myself included, have the burden of proof resting upon him or her. What we put in print may contain errors, but it is based upon the best research available to us at the time of publication. The problem is that we live in a time of mass communication and what would have been a small error may spread so fast and so far that it becomes gospel truth. Historians and researchers can make mistakes.

The most famous of these errors in GAR collecting is the so-called Grand Army Death Badge.

It appeared in a little pamphlet entitled *Collecting GAR Memorabilia* in 1990. The story next appeared in *Civil War Veterans' Organizations, Reunions and Badges* a few years later. It was repeated once more in *American Society Medals* in 1997. It still is not true.

In all the years, I served in the National Sons organization I had never heard of this badge. After reading about it in 1990, a number of us tried to prove it was true that the GAR did issue a Death Badge. However, no records of any kind have been found in support of this fantasy item.

The GAR always wore a black satin or silk ribbon at funerals and on Memorial Day.

So why did this story of a GAR Death Badge appear?

In the 1870s through World War I, a number of military appearing fraternal bodies, with full military garb, were extremely popular. All members of these lodges wore a modified military uniform consisting of jacket, trousers, cape, and bearing swords. Some are gone like the Knights of the Maccabee, but many still exist today like the Knights of Pythias, the Knights of Columbus, the Patriarchs Militant of the Odd Fellows, and the Masonic Knights Templar. All, of course, had an official membership badge.

In 1890, more than 800,000 men were Masons. The Masonic Order known as the Knights Templar was extremely popular. They were often seen in parades with black uniforms and black capes bearing a red cross.

Their official membership badge is still given out to new members today. It consists of a gold edged white enameled cross of Lorraine with an American eagle in the center. The ribbon usually is black, but may be black and white. It sometimes has name bars identifying which Commandery (local chapter) issued it as shown in our example.

A number of Grand Army men were active in the Knights Templar and other fraternal Orders. I am sure they kept their GAR badge & their Knights Templar badge in their jewelry box or dresser drawer. When they died the items were kept together as "Grandpa's old stuff". The author of "Collecting GAR Memorabilia" wrote me "they were found together so many times it couldn't be coincidence".[141]

GAR National Chaplain Horace Carr wearing his GAR, MOLLUS, and Knights Templar badges.

I am afraid it is not only coincidence, but a very confirming statement that many of the veterans loved the military appearing uniforms of these other fraternal orders and joined them. The obituary notices of the veterans themselves often list membership in numerous fraternal orders. The fact that the Knights Templar still issues the same badge today as it did then confirms it's a Knight Templar badge not a GAR Death badge. There are numerous photos of Civil War veterans wearing this Knights Templar badge while they are alive so that statement that it was issued by the GAR upon their death is also disproved. Sadly, some dealers have added even further to the story claiming it as a Lincoln's Funeral badge thus making it even more expensive for the unknowing collector.

The same conclusion was reported in the fall, 1998 issue of *The Veteran*, the Newsletter of the Civil War Veterans Historical Association, in an article entitled "The Death Badge of the GAR Fantasy". It should be noted that other parts of these uniforms have also been listed as Civil War or GAR, such as their kepis and shoulder strap. Beware, and learn the difference between these other lodge uniforms and authentic GAR uniforms.

Other Fantasies

Make believe items are true fantasies. A few years ago some dealers saw an opportunity to make money based upon the popularity of the GAR and the Sons of Veterans. They took the badges and coat of arms of the Sons to Asia and created brand new items - usually badges, belt buckles, or pins - to be sold at flea markets and antique malls. These items are antiqued so they appear old, but are FAKES.

Recently, I saw a round belt buckle that read "GAR Indian Scout". The back was marked "Arizona Territory 1871". Why would the GAR ever produce such an item? They didn't. In the center of the buckle was the official coat of arms of the Sons of Veterans. This coat of arms was patented in 1887, fully 16 years after the date on the buckle. It was a fantasy item created to separate the unsuspecting buyer from his money.

Some collectors and dealers still make fantasy badges from various old parts. These are the hardest to detect because the parts are old.

How do you avoid these costly mistakes? Study and read, then use common sense.

If it's made of the wrong metal, it's not a membership badge. If it's made of gold or silver, it might be a presentation badge made for a past officer. If it's made of pot metal with bronze, gold, silver, or copper wash, it may be a convention or encampment souvenir. Aluminum did exist, but was very rare and expensive then. If the badge has conflicting dates, e.g. the clasp reads 1914, but pendant reads 1921, it is a composite made of old parts. Don't buy it unless you need the parts. Is the manufacturer's name on the reverse and is it the one listed in this book? Beware of strange ribbon colors which indicate replacements.

All Grand Army Orders are federally chartered, and while the GAR badge design is in the public domain today, the designs of the Sons and Loyal Legion are protected by trademark registration.

The legislation that federally incorporated the Sons actually contains the following specified protection: "The corporation (SUVCW) shall have the exclusive right to use…such emblems, seals, and badges as it may legally adopt, and such emblems, seals, and badges as have heretofore been used by the Illinois corporation."… Public Law 605 Chapter 774 Section 17.

In the 1970s fake GAR and Filii Veteranorum badges were coming out of California. It happened again in the 1980s; but the importer was in Virginia. Unknowing or perhaps dishonest antique vendors thinking the GAR and the Sons were long dead, produced cheap metal copies and gave them an antiqued finish.

If the badge details are blurred or do not feel like the correct weight, etc., it is probably one of these fakes. A non-authorized copy of a **Type IV** Sons badge was manufactured in very thin cast aluminum with a black antiquing. On the reverse it appeared bubbled around the coat of arms. It was silver in color, but definitely not the silver plated badge it copied and was issued by a collectors' club. In this case, the plastic pin bar has been riveted in place.

Unfortunately, the plastic bars can be removed and they have been listed in internet auctions as a real pendant. The Sons' pendant appears real until handled. The GAR star was also issued by a collectors' club, but the poor casting immediately gave it away as a fake.

Note the bubbles around the coat of arms on the reverse. This is an indication that the badge is fake.

Again know what to look for so you can spot real from fake.

A note on Reproduction

In a very limited way, the Allied Orders have from time to time made official reproductions of older items, usually for fundraising amongst their members. The Philadelphia version of the Sons of Veterans badge was reissued from the original dies for the 75th anniversary Encampment of the Sons of Union Veterans of Civil War in 1956. It was issued again in 1995 to benefit the GAR Museum of Philadelphia. The one and one-half inch high enameled GAR badge was made by several SUVCW departments and the GAR Museum in Philadelphia, PA. as a recent 1990s fund raiser; it is a desirable collectible, but of new manufacture. Other items have included pins, jewelry, and GAR spoons.

Most reproductions will now carry the words "repro" or the date on the reverse.

They are "official" Allied Orders items, but should not be confused with those made 75 to 100 years ago.

In 2014, the Florida Section of the Order of the Arrow, Boy Scouts of America re-created the 1913 Great Reunion "Scout" badge. The reproduction badge was altered to read 1863-2013 to show it was not the 1913 badge.

The Order of the Arrow founder E. Urner Goodman had been a scoutmaster of one of the 1913 service troops. Mr. Goodman was selected the Scout Executive for the Philadelphia Council in 1917. Here he is shown wearing his Scout version of the Great Reunion Medal.

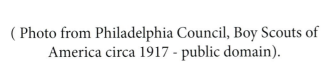

(Photo from Philadelphia Council, Boy Scouts of America circa 1917 - public domain).

Conclusion

All Five of the Allied Orders as well as the Military Order of the Loyal Legion, Dames of the Loyal Legion, and the Daughters of the Union 1861-1865 are still very much alive today. Every year new badges, programs, and proceedings are created. Local, State, and National meetings produce new items. If you had a relative serving in the Union Army, it should be your duty to honor his service by joining one of the Allied Orders.

Many items are still being produced that contain the Grand Army of the Republic badge upon them...especially badges, programs, and ribbons. They are not fakes, just recent additions to the memorabilia produced by the Grand Army family.

Original Design Patents of the male GAR Orders.

Copies can be ordered for a fee from the US Patent Office in Washington, DC:

Grand Army of the Republic

GAR eagle top D016745 June 22, 1886

GAR ribbon #D019189 July 2, 1889

GAR revised badge D016671 May 4, 1886

Sons of Veterans USA

SV Badge Type Ia #D013003 June 27, 1882

Coat of Arms (button/badge) #D0 18740 Nov 20, 1888

SV Camp Seal #D017954 Dec 20, 1887

SV Recognition Pin D017340 May 10, 1887

Military Order of the Loyal Legion

MOLLUS Badge - D017294 May 3, 1887

MOLLUS Lapel button- D018393 Jun 19, 1888

DESIGN.

J. K. DAVISON.

BADGE.

DESIGNSNo. 16,745.

Patented June 22, 1886.

WITNESSES

A. P. Grant

L. Douville

INVENTOR

Joseph K. Davison

BY John A. Biederoheim

ATTORNEY

Badges.

DESIGNS
No. 19,189.

DESIGN.
—o—
J. K. DAVISON.
BADGE.

Patented July 2, 1889.

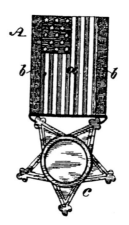

INVENTOR
Joseph K. Davison
BY Diederoheim & Fiutner
ATTORNEYS

194

2

E. A. R.

DESIGNS

No. 16,671.

DESIGN.

J. K. DAVISON.

BADGE.

Patented May 4, 1886.

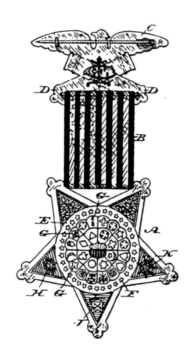

WITNESSES:

A. F. Grant

W. F. Kircher

INVENTOR

Jos. K. Davison

BY

John A. Siedersheim

ATTORNEY

DESIGN.

W. BAILEY & C. E. DAKIN.

BADGE.

No. 13,003.   Patented June 27, 1882.

Fig. 1.

Fig. 2.

Witnesses.   Inventors.
W. W. Mortimer   Wescott Bailey
W. H. Kerr   Chas E. Dakin,
                                                  per
                                              F. A. Lehmann, atty

No. 18,740.

Patented Nov. 20, 1888.

Inventor.

Witnesses.

John C. Snyder

Herbert A. Davis

DESIGNS No. 17,954.

DESIGN.
—o—
A. T. DAVIS.

CAMP SEAL.

Patented Dec. 20, 1887.

Witnesses

Inventor.

DESIGNS,
Fine d.
Badge.
G. A. R.

DESIGN.
—o—
A. P. DAVIS.
BADGE.

DESIGNS No. 17,340.

Patented May 10, 1887.

Witnesses.   Inventor.

W. D. Thomas

H. A. Davis

199

DESIGNS,
Fine Arts,
Badges,
G. A. R.
DESIGNS
No. 17,294.

DESIGN.
—o—
P. D. KEYSER.
BADGE.

Patented May 3, 1887.

OBVERSE.

REVERSE.

WITNESSES
Th Rolle
Jas L. Kelly

INVENTOR
Peter D. Keyser.
BY
John A. Niederstein
ATTORNEY

200

DESIGN.

P. D. KEYSER.

BADGE.

Patented June 19, 1888.

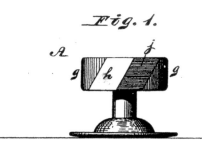

Fig. 1.

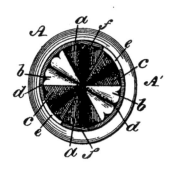

Fig. 2.

WITNESSES:
James P. Kelly.
L. Douville.

INVENTOR:
Peter D. Keyser.
BY Diedersheim Kirchner
ATTORNEYS.

 201

Organization of States by Date

	GAR Organized	Sons Organized	MOLLUS organized
Alabama	March 12,1889	March 12,1889	
Arizonia	Sept. 10,1887		
Arkansas	July 11,1883		
California and Hawaii	Feb. 10,1868	July 1,1886	April 12,1871
Colorado & Wyoming	Dec. 11,1879	1888 / Mar 22,1929	June 1, 1887
Connecticut	April 11,1867	May 15, 1883	
Delaware	Jan. 14,1881		
Florida	June 19,1884	1888	October 27,1973
Georgia	Jan. 25,1889		
Gulf (Louisana)		1888	
Idaho	Sept 1,1887		
Illinois	July 12,1866	July 1883	May 8,1879
Indiana	Oct. 3,1869	June 12, 1885	
Indian Territory & Oklaholma	Aug. 7,1890	May 2, 2002	
Iowa	Jan. 23,1879	June 2,1883	October 20,1886
Kansas	March 16,1880	June, 1883	April 22, 1886
Kentucky	Jan. 17,1883	1888	
Louisiana & Mississippi	May 15,1884		
Maine	Jan. 10,1868	April 10,1883	April 25,1866
Maryland	Jan. 9,1876	June 15 1887	December 8,1904
Massachusetts	May 7, 1867	July 17,1882	March 4,1868
Michigan	Jan. 22, 1879	June 24, 1884	Feb. 4,1885
Minnesota	Aug. 17,1881	Jan. 1,1885	May 6,1885
Missouri	April 22,1882	June 2,1883	Oct. 21,1885
Montana	March 10,1885	1888	
Nebraska	June 11,1877	Sept.2,1885	Oct. 21,1885
New Hampshire	April 30, 1868	Aug 1883	
New Jersey	Dec. 10,1867	June 14,1883	
New Mexico	July 14,1883		
New York	April 3,1867	Nov. 6,1883	Jan. 17,1866
North Dakota	April 23,1890		
Ohio	Jan. 30,1867	Aug. 1,1882	May 3,1882
Oregon	Sept. 28,1882	June 8,1923	May 6, 1885
Pennsylvania	Jan. 16,1867	July 4,1882	April 15,1865
Potomac (Washington,DC)	Feb. 11,1869		Feb. 1,1882
Rhode Island	March 24,1868	Feb 14, 1884	
South Dakota	Feb. 27,1883	1888	
Tennessee	Feb. 26, 1884		
Texas (Southwest)	March 25,1885	2007	October 8,1977
Utah	Oct.19,1883		
Vermont	Oct.23,1868	Oct.,1883	
Virginia	July 27, 1871		
Washington & Alaska	June 20,1883	Jan. 1, 1890	
West Virginia	Feb 20, 1883	1888	
Wisconsin	June 7, 1866	Sept. 1887	May 15,1874

National Encampment Locations

Year	GAR	Sons	Year	GAR	Sons
1866	Indianapolis, IN		1911	Rochester, NY	Rochester, NY
1867	no encampment		1912	Los Angeles, CA	St. Louis, MO
1868	Philadelphia, PA		1913	Chattanooga, TN	Chattanooga, TN
1869	Cincinnati, OH		1914	Detroit, MI	Detroit, MI
1870	Washington, DC		1915	Washington, DC	Washington, DC
1871	Boston, MA		1916	Kansas City, MO	Kansas City, MO
1872	Cleveland, OH		1917	Boston, MA	Boston, MA
1873	New Haven, CT		1918	Portland, OR	Niagara Falls, NY
1874	Harrisburg, PA		1919	Columbus, OH	Columbus, OH
1875	Chicago, IL		1920	Indianapolis, IN	Indianapolis, IN
1876	Philadelphia, PA		1921	Indianapolis, IN	Indianapolis, IN
1877	Providence, RI		1922	Des Moines, IA	Des Moines, IA
1878	Springfield, MA		1923	Milwaukee, WI	Milwaukee, WI
1879	Albany, NY		1924	Boston, MA	Boston, MA
1880	Dayton, OH		1925	Grand Rapids, MI	Grand Rapid, MI
1881	Indianapolis, IN		1926	Des Moines, IA	Des Moines, IA
1882	Baltimore.MD	Pittsburgh, PA	1927	Grand Rapids, MI	Grand Rapid, MI
1883	Denver, CO	Columbus, OH	1928	Denver, CO	Denver, CO
1884	Minneapolis, MN	Philadelphia, PA	1929	Portland, ME	Portland, ME
1885	Portland, ME	Grand Rapids, MI	1930	Cincinnati, OH	Cincinnati, OH
1886	San Francisco, CA	Buffalo, NY	1931	Des Moines, IA	Des Moines, IA
1887	St. Louis, MO	Des Moines, IA	1932	Springfield, IL	Springfield, IL
1888	Columbus, OH	Wheeling, WV	1933	St. Paul, MN	St. Paul, MN
1889	Milwaukee, WI	Patterson, NJ	1934	Rochester, NY	Rochester, NY
1890	Boston, MA	St. Joseph, MO	1935	Grand Rapids, MI	Grand Rapid, MI
1891	Detroit, MI	Minneapolis, MN	1936	Washington, DC	Washington, DC
1892	Washington, DC	Helena, MT	1937	Madison, WI	Madison, WI
1893	Indianapolis, IN	Cincinnati, OH	1938	Des Moines, IA	Des Moines, IA
1894	Pittsburgh, PA	Davenport, IA	1939	Pittsburgh, PA	Pittsburgh, PA
1895	Louisville, KY	Knoxville, TN	1940	Springfield, IL	Springfield, IL
1896	St. Paul, MN	Louisville, KY	1941	Columbus, OH	Columbus, OH
1897	Buffalo, NY	Indianapolis, IN	1942	Indianapolis, IN	Indianapolis, IN
1898	Cincinnati, OH	Omaha, NE	1943	Milwaukee, WI	Milwaukee, WI
1899	Philadelphia, PA	Detroit, MI	1944	Des Moines, IA	Des Moines, IA
1900	Chicago, IL	Syracuse, NY	1945	Columbus, OH	Columbus, OH
1901	Cleveland, OH	Providence, RI	1946	Indianapolis, IN	Indianapolis, IN
1902	Washington, DC	Washington, DC	1947	Cleveland, OH	Cleveland, OH
1903	San Francisco, CA	Atlantic City, NJ	1948	Grand Rapids, MI	Grand Rapid, MI
1904	Boston, MA	Boston, MA	1949	Indianapolis, IN	Indianapolis, IN
1905	Denver, CO	Gettysburg, PA	1950		Boston, MA
1906	Minneapolis, MN	Peoria, IL	1951		Columbus, OH
1907	Sarasota Springs, NY	Dayton, OH	1952		Atlantic City, NJ
1908	Toledo, OH	Niagara Falls, NY	1953		Buffalo, NY
1909	Salt Lake City, UT	Washington, DC	1954		Duluth, MN
1910	Atlantic City, NJ	Atlantic City, NJ	1955		Cincinnati, OH

National Encampment Locations Continued

Year	GAR	Sons	Year	GAR	Sons
1956		Harrisburg, PA	1991		Indianapolis, IN
1957		Detroit, MI	1992		Pittsburgh, PA
1958		Boston, MA	1993		Portland, ME
1959		Long Beach, CA	1994		Lansing, MI
1960		Springfield, IL	1995		Columbus, OH
1961		Indianapolis, IN	1996		Columbus, OH
1962		Washington, DC	1997		Utica, NY
1963		Miami Beach, FL	1998		Harrisburg, PA
1964		Providence, RI	1999		Indianapolis, IN
1965		Richmond, VA	2000		Lansing, MI
1966		Grand Rapids, MI	2001		Springfield, MO
1967		Chicago, IL	2002		Springfield, IL
1968		Wilmington, DE	2003		Ft. Mitchell, KY
1969		St. Louis, MO	2004		Cedar Rapids, IA
1970		Miami Beach, FL	2005		Nashua, NH
1971		Boston, MA	2006		Harrisburg,PA
1972		Philadelphia, PA	2007		St. Louis,MO
1973		Palm Springs, CA	2008		Boston,MA
1974		Bretton Woods, NH	2009		Louisville,KY
1975		Rochester, NY	2010		Overland Park, KS
1976		Columbus, OH	2011		Reston, VA
1977		Des Moines, IA	2012		Los Angeles,CA
1978		Grand Rapids, MI	2013		Milwaukee,WI
1979		Hartford, CT	2014		Marietta,GA
1980		Richmond, VA			
1981		Philadelphia, PA			
1982		Providence, RI			
1983		Portland, ME			
1984		Akron, OH			
1985		Wilmington, DE			
1986		Lexington, KY			
1987		Buffalo, NY			
1988		Lansing, MI			
1989		Stamford, CT			
1990		Des Moines, IA			

ENDNOTES

1 Shaw, Lynn Jackson. *Badges and Ribbons of the United Confederate Veterans and Sons of Confederate Veterans*. N.p.: n.p., c. 1989. 3.

2 Catton, Bruce. "Muffled Roll For Grand Army" *Life*. 20 Aug. 1956. 19.

3 Price, William H. *Civil War Handbook*. Fairfax, VA: Prince Lithograph Co., c. 1961. 2.

4 Cazeau, Theodore. *Annual Report of the Commander-in-Chief, Sons of Union Veterans of the Civil War 1929-1930*. N.p: n.p., n.d. 38.

5 Military Order of the Loyal Legion of the US. *Roster and Constitution and By-Laws of the Military Order of the Loyal Legion of the United States*. N.p.: n.p., 1985. 3-6.

6 Beath, Robert B. *History of the Grand Army of the Republic*. New York, NY: Bryan, Taylor and Co., c. 1888. 22.

7 Carnahan, J. Worth. *Manual of the Civil War and Key to the Grand Army of the Republic and Kindred Societies*. Washington, DC: US Army and Navy Historical Assn., c. 1899. 55-72.

8 Heiple, Roger L. ed. "The Stephenson Papers" *The Great Republic*. South Lyon, MI: GAR Historians and Collectors, c. 1984. Vol 4 # 2, 3, 4.

9 Beath, Robert B. *History of the Grand Army of the Republic*. New York, NY: Bryan, Taylor and Co., c. 1888. 33-50.

10 Beath, Robert B. et al. *The Grand Army Blue Book Edition of 1904*. Philadelphia, PA: J. B. Lippincott Co., c. 1904. 20. "Eligibility to Membership"

11 Grand Army of the Republic. *Ritual of the Grand Army of the Republic*. Indianapolis, IN: Grand Army of the Republic, c. 1921. 12. "Muster-In"

12 Beath, Robert B. et al, *The Grand Army Blue Book Edition of 1904*. Philadelphia, PA: J. B. Lippincott Co., c. 1904. 96. "a resolution adopted at the National Encampment in 1887"

13 Grand Army of the Republic, *Ritual of the Grand Army of the Republic*. Indianapolis, IN: Grand Army of the Republic, c. 1921.

14 Beath, Robert B. et al. *The Grand Army Blue Book Edition of 1904.* Philadelphia, PA: J. B. Lippincott Co., c. 1904. 43-77. "Organization"

15 Dearing, Mary R. *Veterans in Politics: The Story of the GAR.* Baton Rouge: Louisiana State University Press, c. 1952.

16 Beath, Robert B. *History of the Grand Army of the Republic.* New York: Bryan, Taylor and Co., c. 1888. 104. "Politics"

17 Ibid. 98, 101, 119; abolished, 120. Also see *Glorious Contentment* 30-31 for further details.

18 McConnell, Stuart. *Glorious Contentment The Grand Army of the Republic 1865 – 1890.* Chapel Hill, NC: University of North Carolina Press, c. 1992. 28 and 71.

19 Huntington, Tom. "A Monumental Effort" *Preservation.* Summer 2013. Vol. 65 No. 3. 36.

20 Grand Army of the Republic *Journal of the National Encampment.* N.p.: n.p., 1889. 34.

21 Ayers, Edward. "We Will Do Our Best to Take Full Advantage of this Responsibility" *AASLH History News.* Vol. 67 No 1 Winter 2012 Nashville, TN. 18.

22 Grand Army of the Republic *Journal of the National Encampment.* N.p.: n.p., 1889. 71.

23 *Proceedings of the Department of Missouri Second Department Encampment, Grand Army of the Republic 1883.* 21.

24 *Arkansas 23rd Department Encampment Proceedings, Grand Army of the Republic 1905.* 3-4.

25 *New York Times.* August 7, 1891.

26 Gannon, Barbara. *The Won Cause: Black and White Comradeship in the Grand Army of the Republic.* Chapel Hill, NC: University of North Carolina Press, c. 2011. 29.

27 Catton, Bruce. "Muffled Roll For Grand Army" *Life,* 20 Aug. 1956. 20.

28 Beath, Robert B. *History of the Grand Army of the Republic.* New York: Bryan, Taylor and Co., c. 1888. 151.

29 *Official Programme and Directory of the 22nd National Encampment of the Grand Army of the Republic.* Columbus, OH: Press of Nitschke Brothers, c. 1888.

30 Kantor, MacKinlay. "Of Fifes and Drums and The Grand Old Men", *Reader's Digest.* June 1967.

31 Beitler, Lewis. *Report of the Pennsylvania Commission – Fiftieth Anniversary of the Battle of Gettysburg.* Harrisburg, PA: Wm. Ray, State Printer, c. 1915. 216.

32 Ibid. 210.

33 Sons of Union Veterans of the Civil War. "Confirmatory Deed of Conveyance" The Banner Volume 60 # 4 July-August 1956. 1.

34 Vetter, Charles, Charles H. Heimsoth, and John R. Russell. *A Brief History of the Sons of Veterans, USA, General John A. Koltes Camp 171.* New York Sons of Veterans.

35 Sons of Veterans (Post System) *Ritual of the Sons of Veterans Revised 1887.* Albany, NY: C.F. Williams Printing, c. 1887. 13-14.

36 Grand Army of the Republic. *Proceedings of the Twenty-First National Encampment of the Grand Army of the Republic.* held at St. Louis, Missouri September 28-30, 1887.

37 Beath, Robert. *History of the Grand Army of the Republic.* New York, NY: Bryan, Taylor & Company, c. 1888. 229.

38 "The Veterans Sons", Albany, NY: *The Albany Journal.* April 11, 1889.

39 "Sons of Veterans Celebrate", Brooklyn, NY: *Brooklyn Daily Eagle.* August 25, 1889. 16.

40 Davis ★ Camp. *The History of the Order of the Sons of Union Veterans of the Civil War 1881-1939.* N.p.: n.p., c. 1939.

41 "Sons of Army Veterans", New York, NY: *The Daily Graphic.* April 21, 1889. 5.

42 Sons of Veterans, USA. *Constitutions, Rules and Regulations For the Government of the Sons of Veterans, USA Edition of 1882.* N.p.: n. p., [1882]. 8.

43 Davis ★ Camp. *History of the Sons of Union Veterans of the Civil War 1881-1939.* Pittsburgh, PA: n.p., n.d. 14.

44 Sons of Veterans, USA. *Constitutions, Rules and Regulations For the Government of the Sons of Veterans, USA Edition of 1882.* N.p: n.p., [1882]. 80.

45 Sons of Veterans, USA. *Constitutions, Rules and Regulations For the Government of the Sons of Veterans, USA Edition of 1887.* N.p.: n.p., [1887]. 57.

46 Beath, Robert B. *History of the Grand Army of the Republic.* New York, NY: Bryan, Taylor and Co., c. 1888. 237-238.

47 Sons of Veterans, USA. *Constitutions, Rules and Regulations for the Government of the Sons of Veterans. Revised Edition of 1882.* Pittsburgh, PA: John F. Davis, [1882]. 6.

48 Sons of Veterans, USA. *Journal of Proceedings of the Twelfth Annual Encampment of the Sons of Veterans, USA 1893.* Hillsdale, MI: Press of English & Bowman. [1893]. 156.

49 Sons of Veterans, USA. *Constitutions, Rules and Regulations for the Government of the Sons of Veterans, USA. Edition of 1887.* N.p.: n.p., [1887]. Article V "Eligibility to Membership"

50 Ibid. Article VII "Election of Officers"

51 Beath, Robert B. *History of the Grand Army of the Republic.* New York, NY: Bryan, Taylor and Co., c. 1888. 671.

52 Ibid. 672.

53 Sons of Veterans, USA. *The Sons Of Veterans Blue Book* – Digest of Decisions on the Constitution, Rules and Regulations of the Sons of Veterans, USA Compiled by Authority of the Eighth Annual Encampment of the Commandery-in-Chief, Indianapolis, IN: Wm. B. Burford Printer, c. 1890. 79-84.

54 Ibid. 79.

55 Sons of Veterans, USA. *Journal of Proceedings of the Fifth Annual Encampment of the Commandery- in-Chief 1886.* Toledo, OH: Toledo Commercial Book Printing, c. 1886. 30 VII, and 32 III.

56 Beath, Robert B. *History of the Grand Army of the Republic.* New York, NY: Bryan, Taylor and Co., c. 1888. 670.

57 Sons of Veterans, USA. *Journal of Proceedings of the Tenth Annual Encampment of Sons of Veterans, USA.* Topeka, KS: Hamilton Printing, 1891. 58.

58 Sons of Veterans, USA. *Ritual of the Sons of Veterans of the United States of America.* January 1, 1895, Des Moines, IA: Rowen Brothers, [1895]. 17-39.

59 Sons of Veterans, USA. *Ritual of the Sons of Veterans of the United States of America.* January 1, 1897, N.p.: n.p., [1897].

60 Sons of Veterans, USA. *Journal of the Proceedings of the Seventh Annual Encampment of the Commandery-in-Chief 1888.* Chicago, IL: National Reveille, Printers, [1888]. 59.

61 Sons of Veterans, USA. *Rules & Regulations, Sons of Veterans Guards 1892,.*N.p.: n.p., [1892].

62 Sons of Veterans, USA. J*ournal of Proceedings of the Thirteenth Annual Encampment of Sons of Veterans, USA.* Reading, PA.: Press of Reading Review, 1894. 187.

63 Sons of Veterans, USA. General Orders # 2 dated April 12, 1898, Chicago, IL: Commandery-in-Chief Item XII

64 Sons of Veterans, USA. *Roll of Honor of the Sons of Veterans USA.* Boston, MA: EB Stillings & Co., 1899.

65 Sons of Veterans, USA. General Orders # 4 dated September 20, 1898, Chicago, IL: Commandery-in-Chief Item VII.

66 Sons of Veterans, USA. *Proceedings of the Thirty-Ninth Annual Encampment of the Commandery-in- Chief, Sons of Veterans USA.* Dwight, IL: The Banner Print, c. 1920. 203.

67 *Bulletin of Memorial University,* Mason City, IA: Memorial University, June 1908.

68 Sons of Veterans, USA. Circular #2 Series of 1903 dated July 1, 1903 "An Appeal For Memorial University" Indianapolis, IN: Sons of Veterans USA, [1903].

69 Sons of Veterans, USA. *Proceedings of the Thirtieth Annual Encampment Sons of Veterans, USA 1911.* Dwight, IL: Banner Print, [1911]. 42.

70 Gibson, Gary L. ed. *Sons of Union Veterans of the Civil War.* Paducah, KY: Turner Publishing Co., c. 1996. 29.

71 Sons of Veterans, USA. *Constitution and Laws Governing the Sons of Veterans USA Edition of 1905.* N.p.: n.p., [1905]. 15. Article XXIV "Military Department"

72 Sons of Veterans, USA. *The Sons of Veterans Reserve Annual Report 1914.* Gettysburg, PA: Henry Stewart, AAG, [1914].

73 Sons of Veterans, USA. *The Sons of Veterans Reserve Regulations 1917,.* Gettysburg, PA: Henry Stewart, AAG, [1917]. 22.

74 Sons of Veterans, USA. *The Sons of Veterans Reserve Annual Report 1914,* \.Gettysburg, PA: Henry Stewart, AAG, [1914]. 32.

75 Sons of Veterans, USA. *Proceedings of the Thirty-Fourth Annual Encampment of the Commandery-in- Chief.* Dwight, IL: Banner Print, c. 1915. 104-105 "Junior Order Committee Report"

76 Sons of Veterans, USA. *Journal of Proceedings of the Twelfth Annual Encampment of the Sons of Veterans 1893.* Hillsdale, MI: Press of English and Bowman, [1893]. 112-153.

77 Sons of Veterans, USA. *Proceedings Thirty-Third Annual Encampment Commandery-in-Chief Sons of Veterans USA 1914.* Dwight, IL: The Banner Print, [1914]. 32.

78 Sons of Veterans, USA. *Proceedings Thirty-Seventh Annual Encampment Commandery-in-Chief Sons of Veterans USA.* Dwight, IL: The Banner Print, c. 1918. 20.

79 Sons of Union Veterans of the Civil War. *Proceedings Fifty-Third Annual Encampment of the Commandery-in-Chief Sons of Union Veterans of the Civil War.* N.p.: n.p., c. 1934. 49.

80 Ibid.

81 www.fhwa.cot.gov/infrastructure/us6.cfm

82 Sons of Union Veterans of the Civil War. *Proceedings of the One Hundred and Twentieth Annual National Encampment of the Sons of Union Veterans of the Civil War.* held at Springfield, Missouri, N.p.: n.p., August 2001. "Report of the Commander-in-Chief."

83 Green, Kane. "The History of Our Loyal Legion", *The Loyal Legion Bulletin* # 8 March – April 1944

84 Ibid. 1.

85 Commandery of Pennsylvania, *Military Order of the Loyal Legion Fiftieth Anniversary 1915.* 7.

86 *Soldier and Patriots Biographical Album, Chicago*. IL: Union Veteran Publishing Company, c. 1892.

87 Hood, Jennings and Charles Young. *American Orders and Societies and Their Decorations*, Philadelphia, PA: Bailey, Banks and Biddle Company, c. 1917. 69-72. Also, Carroon, Robert and Dana Shoaf. *Union Blue: The History of the Military Order of the Loyal Legion of the United States*. Shippensburg, PA: White Mane Books, c. 2001. 3-25.

88 Military Order of the Loyal Legion. "Recruiting Leaflet", Philadelphia, PA: MOLLUS, c. 1998.

89 Notes on *Decisions of the Commanders-in-Chief of the Military Order of the Loyal Legion of the United States 1865-1889*. Philadelphia, PA: Military Order of the Loyal Legion, 1890.

90 Sons of Union Veterans. *Proceedings Fifty-Third Annual Encampment of the Commandery-in-Chief*. N.p.: n.p., 1934. 14.

91 Ibid. 51.

92 Heiple, Roger, ed. *The Great Republic*. Vol. 1 No. 1 June 1980. South Lyon, MI: GAR Historians & Collectors, [1980]. 2.

93 Beath, Robert B. *History of the Grand Army of the Republic*. New York, NY: Bryan, Taylor and Co., c. 1888. 653.

94 Interview with Roger Heiple, editor *The Great Republic*, organ of the GAR Historians and Collectors Society January 20, 2000.

95 Johnson, Kenneth R. and Jeffrey B. Floyd. *Membership and National Encampment Badges of the Grand Army of the Republic 1866-1949*. Duluth, GA: Order and Medals Society of America Monograph # 11 c. 1997. 3.

96 Beath, Robert B. *History of the Grand Army of the Republic*. New York, NY: Bryan, Taylor and Co., c. 1888. 653.

97 Ibid. 654-655.

98 Page, Charles. January 7, 2005 interview. Mr. Page is the great-nephew of Frederick Starring and owner of this numbered badge.

99 Grand Army of the Republic. *Proceedings of the First to Tenth Meeting of the National Encampment Grand Army of the Republic*. Philadelphia, PA: Samuel Town, c. 1877. "1876 Proceedings"

100 Catalogs of various suppliers 1890-1910 period: Annin, Lilley, Joel, Dettera Flag Co.

101 US Patent Office – Design Patent D 19189 dated July 2, 1889

102 Grand Army of the Republic. *The Grand Army Blue Book Edition of 1904.* Philadelphia, PA: J.B. Lippincott & Co., [1905]. Chapter 5 Article 9 "Badges" p 97

103 US Patent Office – Design Patent D 16671 dated May 4, 1886

104 Beath, Robert B. *History of the Grand Army of the Republic.* New York, New York: Bryan, Taylor and Co., c. 1888. 274.

105 Ibid. 658.

106 Ibid. 293.

107 Ibid. 311.

108 Ibid. 317.

109 Grand Army of the Republic. *The Grand Army Blue Book Edition of 1904.* Philadelphia, PA: J.B. Lippincott & Co, [1904]. Chapter 5 Article 9 Badges. 100-101.

110 Ibid. 98.

111 Joel, J. A. "Special Price list for GAR and S of V Supplies", New York, NY: n.p., c. 1896.

112 Gibson, Gary L. ed. *Sons of Union Veterans of the Civil War.* Paducah, KY: Turner Publishing Co., 1996. 36.

113 Joel, J. A. "Special Price list for GAR and S of V Supplies", New York, NY: n.p., c. 1896.

114 Johnson, Kenneth R. and Jeffrey B. Floyd. *Membership and National Encampment Badges of the Grand Army of the Republic 1866-1949.* Duluth, GA: Order and Medals Society of America Monograph # 11 c. 1997.

115 Grand Army of the Republic. *The Grand Army Blue Book Edition of 1904.* Philadelphia, PA: J.B. Lippincott & Co. Chapter 2 Article 2 p. 30 "Membership is restricted to a single class, and to the exclusion of all others, such as Honorary, Associate or Contributing Memberships".

116 *Rules and Regulations for the Government of the Sons of Veterans*. Brooklyn, NY: Elderidge Print, 1888.

117 Ibid. Article XV Badges

118 Davis, Major A. P. Letter to the Brothers of Davis Camp challenging them to increase membership for the year 1888. dated December 7, 1887, found in Records of Davis ★ Camp, Soldiers and Sailors Hall, Pittsburgh, PA. The Davis challenge covers the next three badges and extends to the Ladies Aid Society Chapter as well. The letter does not state this is a national challenge, but he may have later made it so.

119 Sons of Veterans, USA. *Journal of Proceedings of the Sixth Annual Encampment of the Commandery- in-Chief, Sons of Veterans of the United States of America 1887*. N.p.: n.p., [1887].

120 Ibid. 44.

121 Sons of Veterans, USA. *Constitutions, Rules and Regulations for the Government of the Sons of Veterans, USA Edition 1882*. Article X Section 2

122 Sons of Veterans, USA. *Constitution and Law Governing the Sons of Veterans USA Edition of 1907*. p. 23.

123 Sons of Veterans, USA. *Constitutions, Rules and Regulations for the Government of the Sons of Veterans, USA Edition of 1889*. Chapter VI Art XI Sec 6

124 Sons of Veterans, USA. *Constitution and Laws Governing the Sons of Veterans USA Edition of 1905*. p. 21

125 Shriver, Chester. Personal letter to Robert Wolz, 23 September, 1981.

126 Sons of Veterans, USA. *Proceedings of the Thirty-Thirds Annual Encampment of the Commandery-in-Chief 1914*. Dwight, IL: Banner Print, [1914]. 34.

127 Sons of Veterans, USA. *Constitutions, Rules and Regulations for the Government of the Sons of Veterans, USA Edition of 1882*. N.p.: Grand Divisions, [1882]. 42.

128 Sons of Veterans, USA. *Constitution and Laws Governing The Sons of Veterans Edition of 1912*. N.p.: n.p., [1912] .59.

129 Heiple, Roger, ed. *The Great Republic*. Vol.1 No. 1 June 1980 South Lyon, MI: GAR Historians and Collectors. 8.

130 Sons of Union Veterans of the Civil. *War Constitution & Regulations for the Sons of Union Veterans of the Civil War 1992*. N.p.: n.p., [1992].

131 Sons of Veterans, USA. *The Sons of Veterans Reserve Regulations 1917,*. Gettysburg, PA: Henry Stewart, [1917].

132 Sons of Union Veterans of the Civil War. *The Sons of Veterans Reserve Regulations 1960*. Gettysburg, PA: NMD, SVR, [1960]. Also, Sons of Union Veterans of the Civil War. *The Sons of Veterans Reserve Regulations 1979*. New Waterford, Ohio: Robert Wolz, TAG,NMD,SVR, [1979].

133 Pennsylvania Department, Sons of Union Veterans of the Civil War. Regulations Governing the Uniform of the Military Dept Sons of Union Veterans of the Civil War – Sons of Veterans Reserve – Penn. Dept. Dated Feb. 25, 1922. Col. S. S. Horn, Chairman p. 4

134 Sons of Veterans, USA. *The Sons of Veterans Reserve Regulations 1917*. Gettysburg, Pa: Henry Stewart, [1917].

135 Sons of Union Veterans of the Civil War. *The Banner.* Volume 102 No. 1 September 1997. Lititz, PA c. 1997. 11.

136 Military Order of the Loyal Legion of the United States. *Constitution and Bylaws*. N.p.: n.p., 2010.

137 US Patent Office Design Patent # D 17,294 dated May 3, 1887

138 Military Order of the Loyal Legion of the United States. *Roster and Constitution and By-laws of the Military Order of the Loyal Legion of the United States Edition of 1985*. p. 8 "Insignia of the Order"

139 Foering, John, recorder-in-Chief. *Constitution and By-laws 1929*. Philadelphia, PA: MOLLUS, [1929]. 28-29.

140 US Patent Office Design Patent D18,393 dated June 19, 1888

141 E-mail dated 13 January 1999 with Brad Long, author *Collecting GAR Memorabilia*. Also "Death Badge of the GAR Fantasy" *The Veteran.* Vol.12 No. 1 Fall, 1998 South Lyon. MI p.10.

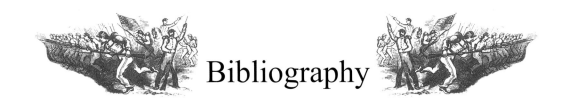

Bibliography

Albany Journal. "The Veterans Sons" Albany, NY: Apr 11, 1889. Print.

Ashbrook, John M. "The 100th Anniversary of the Grand Army of the Republic." *Congressional Record 89th Congress* 2nd Session April 6, 1966 Washington, DC: Government Printing Office, 1966. Print.

The Banner. Journal of the Sons of Union Veterans of the Civil War. Various issues 1939 to present. Print.

Beath, Robert. *History of the Grand Army of the Republic.* New York, NY: Bryan, Taylor & Co, 1888. Print.

Bishop, Lee and J. Robert Elliott. *American Society Medals An Identification Guide.* Santa Monica, CA: Bishop & Elliott Publications, n.d. Print.

Blue Book of the Grand Army of the Republic. Philadelphia, PA: JB Lippincott Co., 1904. Print.

Blue Book of the Sons of Veterans of the United States of America. Indianapolis, IN: Wm. B. Burford, 1890. Print.

Brooklyn Daily Eagle. "Sons of Veterans Celebrate" Brooklyn, NY: Aug 25, 1889. Print.

Carnahan, J. Worth. *Manual of the Civil War and Key to the Grand Army of the Republic and Kindred Societies.* Washington, DC: US Army & Navy Historical Assn., 1899. Print.

Carroon, Robert and Dana Shoaf. Union Blue: *The History of the Military Order of the Loyal Legion of the United States.* Shippensburg, PA: White Mane Publishers, 2001. Print.

Catton, Bruce. "Muffled Roll for Grand Army" *Life Magazine.* Vol 41 No 8, 20 Aug. 1956. Print.

Constitution of the Sons of Union Veterans of the Civil War. N.p.: n.p., Editions of 1925, 1939, 1956, 1997, 2000, 2002. Print.

Constitution of the Sons of Veterans of the United States of America. N.p.: n.p., Editions of 1882, 1889, 1891, 1893, 1902, 1905, 1912 & 1920. Print.

Dearing, Mary R. *Veterans in Politics: The Story of the GAR*. Baton Rouge, LA: Louisiana State University Press, 1952. Print.

Decisions of the Commandery-in-Chief, Military Order of the Loyal Legion 1865-1889. Philadelphia, PA: n.p., 1890. Print.

Gannon, Barbara A. *The Won Cause: Black and White Comradeship in the Grand Army of the Republic*. Chapel Hill, NC: University of North Carolina Press, 2011. Print.

Grand Army of the Republic. *Journal of the National Encampment*. N.p.: Various journals 1881,1883,1887,1888,1904,1914,1915, 1925, 1927, 1934, 1949. Print.

Gregg, Dennis. *A Collector's Identification and Price Guide for Grand Army of the Republic Memorabilia*. Funkstown, MD: Full House Publications, 2005. Print.

Gibson, Gary L. ed. *Sons of Union Veterans of the Civil War*. Paducah, KY: Turner Publishing Co., 1996. Print.

Gould, Edward K. *Sons of Veterans Digest*. Rockland, ME: Press of the Courier-Gazette, 1897. Print.

---*Sons of Veterans Guide*. Rockland, ME: Press of the Courier-Gazette. 1885. Print.

---*Sons of Veterans Guide for Officers and Members of the Sons of Veterans USA and Ladies Aid Societies 2nd Revised Edition*. Rockland, ME: Press of the Courier-Gazette. 1888. Print.

Hall, Marvin. Price List Sons of Veterans and Military Goods. Hillsdale, MI: n.p., c. 1890.Print.

Heiple, Roger. *The Great Republic*. South Lyon, MI: GAR Historians & Collectors, various issues, 1983-1985. Print.

Hood, Jennings and Charles Young. *American Orders and Societies and Their Decorations*. Philadelphia, PA: Bailey, Banks and Biddle, 1917. Print.

Huntington, Tom. A Monumental Effort. *Preservation Magazine*. Vol 65 No 3. summer 2013.

Joel, J.A., Special Price list for GAR and S of V Supplies. New York, NY: n.p., c. 1896. Print.

Johnson, Kenneth & Jeffery Floyd. *Membership & National Encampment Badges of the Grand Army of the Republic, 1866-1949*. Glassboro, NJ: Orders & Medals Society of America, 1997. Print.

Journal of Proceedings of the Eleventh Annual Encampment of Sons of Veterans, USA. Topeka, KS: Hamilton Printing, 1892. Print.

Journal of Proceedings of the Fifth Annual Encampment of Commandery-in-Chief, Sons of Veterans, USA. Toledo, OH: Toledo Commercial Book Printing, 1886. Print.

Journal of Proceedings of the Seventh Annual Encampment of the Commandery-in-Chief, Sons of Veterans of the United States of America. Chicago, IL: National Reveille, 1888. Print.

Journal of Proceedings of the Tenth Annual Encampment of Sons of Veterans, USA. Topeka, KS: Hamilton Printing, 1891. Print.

Journal of Proceedings of the Thirteenth Annual Encampment of Sons of Veterans, USA. Reading, PA.: Press of Reading Review, 1894. Print.

Journal of Proceedings of the Twelfth Annual Encampment of Sons of Veterans, USA. Hillsdale, MI: Press of English & Bowman, 1893. Print.

Kantor, MacKinlay. *Readers Digest*. "Of Fifes & Drums & The Grand Old Men" June 1967. Print.

Kinnaird, Clark. *First Century 1866-1966 and Forward*. Kingsport. TN: Commandery of the State of New York Military Order of the Loyal Legion, USA, 1966. Print.

Kirkland, Turner. *Civil War Veterans' Organizations. Reunions and Badges*. Union City, TN: Pioneer Press c.1991. Print.

Long, R. Brad. *Collecting Grand Army of the Republic Memorabilia*. Martinsville, IL: Pap-R Products Printing, 1990. Print.

McConnell, Stuart. *Glorious Contentment: The Grand Army of the Republic 1865-1900*. Chapel Hill, NC: University of North Carolina, 1992. Print.

Military Order of the Loyal Legion of the United States Ceremonies for the Twenty-Fifth Anniversary. Philadelphia, PA: April 1890. Print.

Military Order of the Loyal Legion of the United States Constitution and Bylaws. Philadelphia, PA: Editions 1885, 1929, 1964, 1989 & 2010. Print.

Nicholson, John. *Military Order of the Loyal Legion of the United States Ceremonies for the Fiftieth Anniversary*. Philadelphia, PA: April 1915. Print.

Price, William. *Civil War Handbook*. Fairfax, VA: Prince Lithograph, 1961. Print.

Proceedings of the 17th Annual Encampment, Ohio Division, Sons of Veterans, USA. Columbus, OH: Daily Express, 1899. Print.

Proceedings of the First to Tenth Meeting of the National Encampment Grand Army of the Republic. Philadelphia, PA: Samuel Town, 1877. Print.

Proceedings of the Thirty-Fifth Annual Encampment of the Commandery-in-Chief, Sons of Veterans, USA. Dwight, IL: Banner Print, 1916. Print.

Ritual, Grand Army of the Republic. N.p.: n.p., Editions 1911 and 1921. Print.

Ritual, Sons of Veterans (post system). Albany, NY: C.C.Williams, 1887. Print.

Ritual, Sons of Veterans, USA & Sons of Union Veterans. N.p: n.p., Editions 1889,

Editions 1891, 1895, 1899, 1911 1920, 1925, 1926, 1956, 1966. Print.

Roll of Honor of the Sons of Veterans, USA. Boston, MA: E.B. Stillings & Co., 1899. Print.

Roy, Paul. *The Last Reunion of the Blue and Gray.* Gettysburg, PA: Gettysburg Times, 1950. Print.

Rules & Regulations of Sons of Veterans (post System). Brooklyn, NY: Elderidge Print, 1888. Print.

Rules & Regulations of the Grand Army of the Republic. N.p.: n.p., Editions 1887, 1907, 1922. Print.

Rules & Regulations, Sons of Veterans Guards. N.p.: Sons of Veterans USA, 1892. Print.

Shaw, Lynn. *Badges & Ribbons of the United Confederate Veterans and the Sons of Confederate Veterans.* N.p.: n.p., c.1988. Print.

Soldier and Patriots Biographical Album. Chicago, IL: Union Veterans Publishing Company, 1892. Print.

Sons of Veterans Reserve Annual Report 1914. Gettysburg, PA: Henry Stewart, AAG, [1914]. Print.

Sons of Veterans Reserve Regulations 1917. Gettysburg, PA: Henry Stewart, AAG, [1917]. Print.

Sons of Veterans Reserve Regulations 1960. N.p.; n.p., [1960]. Print.

Sons of Veterans Reserve Regulations 1979. New Waterford, OH: Robert Wolz, TAG, NMD, SVR. [1979]. Print.

Tuttle, Craig. *An Ounce of Preservation: A Guide to the Care of Papers & Photographs.* Highland City, FL: Rainbow Books, 1994. Print.

Vetter, Charles, Charles Heimsoth, and John A. Russell. *A Brief History of the Sons of Veterans, USA Koltes Camp # 171, New York Division.* N.p.: n.p., c. 1899. Print.

INDEX

Other Books by the Author

- *Presidents in Paradise: The legacy of the Little White House*

- *Israel and the Legacy of Harry S. Truman*

- *The National Security Legacy Of Harry S. Truman*

All pictures Courtesy of the Library of Congress and the Journal of the GAR National Encampments

"Keep green in our minds the memory of those ... who sacrificed so much that the life of the nation might be preserved, and deal with them in all things with Thy special mercy."

SV, USA Ritual 1895

All pictures Courtesy of the Library of Congress and the Journal of the GAR National Encampments

All pictures Courtesy of the Library of Congress and the Journal of the GAR National Encampments

Courtesy of the Library of Congress and Journal of the GAR National Encampments